P9-CLR-640

THE JESUS OF SUBURBIA

THE JESUS OF SUBURBIA

Have We Tamed the Son of God to Fit Our Lifestyle?

MIKE ERRE

W PUBLISHING GROUP

A Division of Thomas Nelson Publishers

Since 1798

www.wpublishinggroup.com

THE JESUS OF SUBURBIA
Copyright © 2006 Mike Erre

All rights reserved. No portion of this book may be reproduced, stored in a retrieval system, or transmitted in any form or by any means—electronic, mechanical, photocopy, recording, or any other—except for brief quotations in printed reviews, without the prior written permission of the publisher.

Published by W Publishing Group, a Division of Thomas Nelson, Inc., P.O. Box 141000, Nashville, Tennessee, 37214.

W Publishing Group books may be purchased in bulk for educational, business, fundraising, or sales promotional use. For information, please email SpecialMarkets@ThomasNelson.com.

All Scripture quotations, unless otherwise indicated, are taken from *The Holy Bible*, New International Version (NIV). Copyright © 1973, 1978, 1984. International Bible Society. Used by permission of Zondervan Bible Publishers..

Editorial Staff: Greg Daniel, acquisitions editor, and Thom Chittom, managing editor
Cover Design: Gearbox Design
Page Design: Walter Petrie

Library of Congress Cataloging-in-Publication Data

Erre, Mike, 1971–
    The Jesus of suburbia / Mike Erre.
        p. cm.
    Includes bibliographical references and index.
    ISBN-10: 0-8499-0059-X
    ISBN-13: 978-0-8499-0059-4
    1. Christian life. I. Title.
BV4501.3.E73 2006
248.4—dc22   2006012968

Printed in the United States of America

06 07 08 09 10 RRD 5 4 3 2 1

This book is dedicated to my wife, Justina: "Like a lily among thorns is my darling among the maidens" (Song of Songs 2:2). You are God's blessing to me.

CONTENTS

Acknowledgments   ix

Introduction   xi

1. Revolution   1
2. The Narrow Road   21
3. The Failure of Religion   39
4. The Scandal of Grace   57
5. The Danger of Theology   77
6. All Things Are Spiritual   97
7. Mystery and Paradox   115
8. The Church As Subversive Community   135
9. The Redemption of Culture   153
10. Show and Tell   175

Notes   197

ACKNOWLEDGMENTS

This book has been formed in a community of many men and women who help inspire and sharpen. Thank you to:

Bruce and Stan—for dreaming up Isaachar and inviting me along for the ride

Greg Daniel—for taking a risk on me and for much helpful critique

Mark Sweeney—for believing in me and this book

Todd Proctor—for the joy of going to war with you, time and again

Chad Halliburton, Pete Shambrook, and Nick Taylor—for walking with me in dark places

The Elders, Staff, and Revolutionaries of Rock Harbor Church—for allowing me the freedom to learn, stumble, and grow in front of you

Donna Wells—for your tireless care and diligence

Krysti Hall—for some fantastic, last-minute spit and polish

My folks—for much love and support

Nathaniel and Hannah Erre—for teaching me more about God's love than I could have imagined

Erwin McManus, Rich Nathan, Rob Bell, Kenton Beshore, Dallas Willard, Bart Tarman, JP Moreland—mentors far and near whose thinking has dramatically shaped my own. I have learned to see Jesus more clearly through your work, and I hope I've given you enough credit in this book. Your ideas have stayed with me for so long that I've given up the temptation to think that I've ever had an original thought.

Introduction

I absolutely love Jesus Christ. I don't think he is a figment or a crutch or some religious hangover. I think he is real and alive and wonderfully engaged in the world today. But I have serious problems with the religion that bears his name. As a pastor, I have been a follower of Christ as well as a follower of Christianity. And I can't help but notice there is a growing difference between the two. (Maybe that difference has always been there and I've just never seen it until now. Maybe each new generation must come to grips with this difference, as the church grows increasingly removed from its founder.)

I am also a big fan of the Bible. I love that it is raw, inspiring, convicting, living, and terrifying all at the same time. I love that it is honest. I find it fascinating that, in the second chapter of Luke, we read about Jesus's parents returning home from a Passover feast in Jerusalem—without him! They left him behind in the city and walked an entire day without noticing that he was missing. When he didn't turn up, the Bible says, they became worried and started looking for him. No kidding. They'd just misplaced the Savior of the world!

To be fair to Mary and Joseph, in those days people traveled in large groups for protection . . . but still.

And so for a while, anyway, Jesus's parents lost the Messiah. Unknowingly, they had moved on without him. Once they realized this, they spent the next three days looking for him, only to find him back in the temple (where, Jesus implied, they should have known they would find him all along).

This story brings to mind much of modern American Christianity. It seems in many ways we are like Jesus's parents on the road to Jerusalem: we think he is with us, but we've moved on without him. We preach Christianity, but do we really preach Christ? We call people to serve the church, but do we call them to serve the poor? We teach them to know sound doctrine, but do we teach people to center their whole lives (and not just their intellectual knowledge) on him? Do we teach people to have a commitment to the Bible or to a relationship with its author?

I think we may have lost sight of Jesus among all the trappings of the Christian religion. Amid all the hype about the growing political power of evangelicals, the growing numbers of mega-churches, and the booming, billion-dollar Christian subculture industry, I wonder if we have left Jesus behind. Or, worse, if he has left us behind. Either way, I think the story in Luke 2 is a fitting picture of where we find ourselves with Christianity today in the West.

I am not alone in noticing this. Growing numbers of people are awakening to the same thought Mary and Joseph must have had: we've lost Jesus, and we need to begin searching for him.

Without question, Jesus can still be found "in [his] father's house," the church. He's just not so easy to spot these days. We cower behind our fortress of absolute truth, arrogantly pronouncing judgment on the world around us, condemning sin and sinner alike. Dare we consider the possibility that Jesus might be preaching a different message, to a different audience, in a different way than the message we have embraced as the American church? Like Mary and Joseph recognized, it is time to become worried and to begin searching for him.

The search begins with tough questions. Do we as Western Christians reflect Jesus or obscure him? Can we say that we, his church, teach what he taught, love what (and whom) he loved, and hate what he hated? Are his priorities really ours?

My primary contention is this: Much of what passes for modern, western Christianity isn't of Jesus. We can (and do) lose Jesus right in the middle of prayer meetings and worship services. We can miss him in the Bible and in the church. As the Scriptures remind us, not all worship is pleasing to God, not all church services are attended by Jesus, not all teaching is sound teaching, and not all prayer is "in Jesus's name."

Why is it that:

- Study after study shows no statistical difference between the behaviors of those inside the church and those outside it?

- So many Christians have adopted a "victim mentality" with an attitude of helplessness and have put much of our hope and trust in the political process and court system, implying that God's work on earth depends upon who sits in the White House?

- We currently see very little of the power, vitality, and growth today in our hearts and churches that once characterized the explosive movement of God?

Is it because we have substituted human traditions for the teachings of God? Have we made our Jesus the Jesus of Christianity, not the Jesus of the Gospels? We may think we worship the Jesus of Nazareth, but in reality we worship the Jesus of Suburbia.

At first glance, the Jesus of Suburbia bears a resemblance to the real Jesus who walked the earth commanding his followers to deny themselves, bless those who persecute them, and love their enemies. But the real difference between the two becomes plain once we are actually asked to live that way, not just passively agree with the sentiment of the words.

The suburban Jesus would never be so offensive as to demand that we do what he says: he is more interested in the security, comfort, and prosperity of his followers. In short, much of the message of American Christianity presents Jesus as the purveyor of the American Dream.

Such a counterfeit can never stand against the real thing. Perhaps the church has been lulled into complacency by years of the very things we point to as proofs of God's blessing upon America: religious freedom and material abundance. We have never really embraced the message and movement of Jesus Christ as a call to revolution. Instead, we have gotten comfortable with a watered-down, whitewashed, religiously safe version of him. Like many others, I have begun to realize my own idolatry and cowardice in this regard.

This book is my attempt to add to the centuries-old conversation about the working out of the message of Jesus in each new generation. I want to raise questions and make the case that this non-Christian Christianity will never satisfy, never revive the church, and never transform the lives of men and women who so desperately need him. We must each acknowledge the places and ways where we have substituted the suburban Jesus for the real thing. And we have to walk courageously away from the false security of the imposter if we hope ever to know the power and danger of the genuine Christ.

I am also guilty of missing the revolution of Jesus. I embraced Christianity but missed Jesus Christ. I am a pastor at a wonderful church but have lost sight of him even there.

I lost him right in the middle of all the stuff that I was supposedly doing in his name. I have become worried and have started looking for him. And I am learning to find him, just like Mary and Joseph, right where I should have expected him to be all along.

1

REVOLUTION

My two-and-a-half-year-old son loves animals. He loves to see them, make their sounds, and watch them in action. Seeing his interest and enjoyment, my wife and I decided to take him to the Wild Animal Park near San Diego. The Wild Animal Park isn't a zoo, exactly; it's more about wide-open spaces. Instead of a maze of fenced cages, the park is sectioned off into representative regions of the world, in which most of the animals roam freely. Can you see why we thought this would captivate our little boy?

Right near the park entrance sits a gift shop. All glassy and shiny, it lured our boy right in. We spent what seemed like forever in the gift shop watching Nathan play with plastic elephants, lions, and giraffes. We kept reminding him that *real* elephants, lions, and giraffes awaited inside the park, but he was content to play in the gift shop. As my frustration with my son grew (Didn't he know we paid twenty-five dollars a

1

head and drove an hour and a half on my day off for him to see the *real* animals?), I realized I have often done the very thing my son was doing.

I grew up in the Midwest. For summer break each year, my stepfather and mother would take my brother and me around the West in a forty-foot RV for several weeks at a time. We would see the most incredible sights: Yosemite, Yellowstone, Glacier National Park, and the Grand Canyon. But to my brother and me, the most important thing about each stop along the way was whether or not the campground had a swimming pool. Seriously. We were traveling the country looking at some of the most beautiful stuff in the world, and all we worried about was whether or not we could go for a swim. My folks couldn't believe it. They would have to force us out of the pool to go see the Grand Canyon; we would have been content without seeing it all.

As I stood there looking at my little boy and being reminded of my own childhood, a quote from C. S. Lewis came to mind: "It would seem our Lord finds our desires, not too strong, but too weak. . . . We are far too easily pleased."[1] This is so true of my little boy and me. There is nothing wrong with gift shops and campground swimming pools, but in light of what we were missing by choosing those things, our desires were weak and myopic. My son settled for the gift shop animals instead of the real ones; I was content with the swimming pool rather than the Grand Canyon.

The spiritual parallels are obvious, and this is what C. S.

Lewis was getting at. Far too many of us settle for the gift shop/swimming pool Jesus than the real thing. We are drawn to the Jesus of Suburbia—the tame, whitewashed, milquetoast Jesus who is primarily interested in our security and comfort—and oblivious to the dangerous and wild Jesus of Nazareth who beckons us beyond the safety of our small lives.

We must constantly guard against the counterfeit Jesus who pervades our culture and churches. The real one is far bigger and more dangerous than we realize. We must consciously resist the temptation to tone him down or soften his teachings, or we may miss him altogether.

Nowhere does the Christian community succumb to the gift shop Jesus more than during the Christmas season. Sure, we tell the manger narrative and defend our rights to say "Merry Christmas," but on the whole, the story we tell is pretty toned down. It is so familiar that it has lost its power. We have heard it so much that the idea of God in a manger no longer inspires awe and humility. We don't talk much about Jesus being such a threat to King Herod that he slaughtered innocent children. We don't talk much about the scandal surrounding Jesus's birth because Mary and Joseph weren't married. We don't talk much about the threat the birth of Jesus posed to the political order of things. These are not part of the eggnog, mistletoe, Frosty-the-Snowman Christmas story we have come to know.

Jesus's birth was revolution. It changed everything. There

is no better place to begin our war against the counterfeit Jesus of Suburbia than with the birth of the real one.

Two Kingdoms

This is the first sentence in Luke's account of the birth of Jesus: "In those days Caesar Augustus issued a decree that a census should be taken of the entire Roman world" (Luke 2:1). I have always read this as a passing, incidental reference to Caesar that sets up the reason Joseph and Mary had to travel to Bethlehem. That's all I thought it was. But a closer look reveals that this information is far from incidental: Luke is revealing a backdrop that brings the birth of Jesus into sharp relief.[2]

As most of us learned in high school (and many of us forgot very shortly thereafter), Julius Caesar was murdered in 44 BC because in the eyes of many in the Roman Senate he had become too powerful. Before his death, Julius adopted his grandnephew Octavian and named him heir. After the murder of Julius Caesar, Octavian did three things. First, he adopted his father's family name, *Caesar*. Second, he determined to kill his father's murderers, setting the stage for the decade-long civil war that would engulf the Roman Empire. And third, he staged elaborate public games in honor of his adopted father. During the course of these games, a comet appeared—an event that was viewed by the people of that time as a fortuitous sign. Octavian pointed to the comet as proof of his adopted father's divinity; this was the sign that Julius ascended after his death into heaven to sit at the right hand of the god Zeus. Octavian used this against his political enemies; if his father was a god, what did that make him? A son of god. We have records of coins and inscriptions that Octavian used to call himself "son of the deified one."[3]

For over a decade, civil war waged as Octavian and his allies warred against his enemies. Civil war engulfed Rome and the rest of the known world with it. When Octavian defeated his main rival, Mark Antony, in the battle of Actium in 31 BC, peace was restored to the Empire. Octavian rose to power, hailed as the "bringer of peace." Priests were instructed to include his name in all prayers and vows, and his birthday and the date of his victory became national holidays.

Soon after this, Octavian received the honorific title *Augustus* ("the illustrious one"), naming him as unique among all Romans. He came to be known as the "Savior" of the empire, bringing "peace" and "salvation." He was called the "Lord" and came to be worshiped as a god on earth. Roman citizens were commanded to pray to him and offer sacrifices. Temples and shrines were built in his name. Monuments all over the empire listed his accomplishments. Games were held in his honor. His birth was called "good news" and was celebrated by a twelve-day holiday called "advent." Among his titles were: "Cosmic Savior," "Atonement for Rome's Past Sins," and "Inaugurator of the Golden Age of Peace and Security."

He was savior, and his kingdom was salvation. The propaganda spilling forth from Rome announced the "good news" of Augustus's birth and that the blessing of Caesar's kingdom was peace. This peace, of course, came at the point of a sword and was most definitely not good news for Rome's enemies. An inscription dated 9 BC gives us a glimpse of the honor and worship that was accorded Caesar Augustus by the people of Rome:

> The most divine Caesar . . . we should consider equal to the Beginning of all things . . . for when everything was falling [into disorder] and tending toward dissolution, he restored it once more and gave to the whole world a new aura; Caesar . . . the common good Fortune of all . . . The beginning of life and vitality . . . All the cities unanimously adopt the birthday of the divine Caesar as the new beginning of the year . . . Whereas Providence, which has regulated our whole existence . . . has brought our life to the climax of perfection in giving to us [the emperor] Augustus, whom it [Providence] filled with strength for the welfare of men, and who being sent to us and our descendants as Savior, has put an end to war and has set all things in order; and having become god manifest, Caesar has fulfilled all the hopes of earlier times . . . in surpassing all the benefactors who preceded him . . . and whereas, finally, the birthday of the god [Augustus] has been for the whole world the beginning of good news (*euangelion*) concerning him [therefore let a new era begin from his birth].[4]

Many had to take oaths to Caesar and his children and defend his interests even at the cost of their own lives. We have an inscription of such an oath from the region of Galatia:

> At the command of Caesar Augustus, the son of God, I swear by Zeus, the Earth, the Sun, and by all the gods and goddesses including Augustus himself, to be favorable to Caesar Augustus, his sons and descendants forever in speech, in actions, and in thoughts, considering as friends those he considers so, and regarding as enemies those he judges so, and to defend their interests I will spare neither body, nor soul, nor life, nor my children.[5]

Allegiance to Caesar was both political and religious for the people of the Roman Empire. It was not enough to honor him as Emperor; he demanded to be worshiped as "god" also.

Luke's mention of Caesar Augustus isn't incidental or minor. It sets the whole backdrop for the Christmas story. The census ordered by Augustus was one of the ways he controlled the Roman Empire. By demanding taxes (or tribute, more specifically), Caesar could provide for his far-flung armies as well as humiliate the peoples under Roman "peace" by reminding them they lived at the will of Rome.

Luke wants us to know that there is a bigger stage than we realize for the birth of Jesus Christ. In one corner of this massive empire, Luke recorded for us the birth of a new king, ushering in a new and revolutionary kind of kingdom. The world lived under the rule of Caesar Augustus, yet Luke wanted us to know that hundreds of miles away, something so significant was happening that it would shake every empire and affect every life from that day to today. With this historical background in mind, the announcement by the angels made to the shepherds becomes stunning:

> And there were shepherds living out in the fields nearby, keeping watch over their flocks at night. An angel of the Lord appeared to them, and the glory of the Lord shone around them, and they were terrified. But the angel said to them, "Do not be afraid. I bring you good news of great joy that will be for all the people. Today in the town of David a Savior has been born to you; he is Christ the Lord." . . . Suddenly a great company of the heavenly host appeared with the angel, praising God and saying, "Glory to God in the highest, and on earth peace to men on whom his favor rests." (Luke 2:8–11, 13–14)

This is simply amazing. It was said that *Caesar* was Savior, Lord, and bringer of peace. *His* birthday was good news, and *his* empire was salvation. And here, in a corner of the most powerful kingdom the world had ever seen, shepherds (not priests, not rulers, not the elite) were the first to hear the good news that will be for *all people* (not just the wealthy and the powerful). A different Savior, Lord, and King will usher in a real peace and lasting salvation.

The announcement in Luke's gospel is the announcement of a king born in *direct opposition* to the rule and reign of Caesar. It is almost as if all the titles applied to Caesar were applied to Jesus in order to force people to choose between them. If Jesus had been called one thing and Caesar another, people would have been tempted to believe they could worship both. But when *Savior, Lord, King, gospel, peace* and *salvation* are specific descriptions applied to both rulers, the Christmas story forces us to choose: Who is our Lord? Who is our Savior?

The differences between these two saviors could not be overstated. Augustus's rule was defined by the sword, the shield, and the banners of his legions. The kingdom of Jesus of Nazareth was marked by a manger, a cross, and a tomb. No greater contrast could be imagined. The birth of Jesus Christ was simply revolution: the birth of a different king, ushering in a differing kingdom, and threatening the kingdoms of this world.

Two different empires were established on the day of Jesus's birth. One built on power, the other on love. One built on control, the other on freedom. One built on oppression and bondage, the other on liberation. Augustus was the embodiment of the best the world in all its ambition and lust can offer, a ruler who sat at the apex of a world-wide system of worship and domination. Jesus, on the other hand, was destined to humble himself on a tree, sacrificing himself out of love. Jesus represents the dangerous alternative to the power of this world: a different power, a different glory, a different peace, and a different salvation. The Christmas story ceases to be an idyllic myth: it becomes clear these two empires are destined to collide. The birth of Jesus is divine insurrection and outright revolution.

The Christmas story forces us to choose between these two kingdoms. Do we bow before the Caesars of our time, or dare we embrace the kingdom of Jesus?

Two Kings

Matthew records for us the other king mentioned in the Christmas story: Herod the Great.[6] Herod was called the "king of the Jews" and was a puppet king of Rome. He was half Jewish and came from the region of Idumaea. The Senate installed Herod as king in 40 BC, but it took him three years (and several Roman legions) to subdue his subjects. The Jews hated Herod—not only because he was aligned with Rome (and built many monuments, buildings, and even cities dedicated to Caesar Augustus), but also because they saw him as an illegitimate Jewish king.

Herod was cruel even beyond ancient standards. He was suspicious of everyone and went to great lengths to hold on to power. He inaugurated a secret police made up of informants and torturers who would put down any insurgencies. He began the systematic extermination of any who would threaten his power. He had ten wives and had his favorite wife, Mariamme, murdered when he became jealous of her. He murdered three of his sons (all were in line for the throne at the time of his murder) and drowned the high priest of Israel (and one of his brothers-in-law) in the family pool on vacation. He impoverished the Jewish people in order to build massive, extravagant fortresses, cities, and palaces for himself and even financed celebrations and festivals in foreign cities in honor of Augustus. King Herod ruled with such cruelty and ambition that, when he was dying, he ordered many elite Jews be held captive in Jericho and murdered upon his death so that there would be mourning in Israel that day, even if it wasn't for him. This was King Herod: monumentally ambitious and capable, yet cruel and tyrannical.

We read in Matthew 2 that "Magi from the east came to Jerusalem and asked, 'Where is the one who has been born king of the Jews? We saw his star in the east and have come to worship him.' When King Herod heard this he was disturbed, and all Jerusalem with him" (Matt. 2:1–3).

"Disturbed" must have been an understatement. No wonder Herod was disturbed. This was not a man who would take a threat to his kingship lightly—particularly another king called "the king of the Jews." Because Herod was an Idumaean, he would have been particularly sensitive to news of the promised king the Jews were expecting. Further background helps us better understand Herod's concern.

In Genesis 25, Rachel (Isaac's wife) is told that the two sons in her womb will turn into two nations, that those nations will be in conflict with each other, and that the older will serve the younger. Esau was born first and was given his name because he was hairy. Elsewhere in the Bible, Esau is called "Edom," which means "red," because he was born with thick red hair. Jacob was the youngest and later in the Scriptures is renamed Israel. Esau became the father of the Edomites, and Jacob the father of the Israelites.

When the word "Edom" is translated into Greek, it becomes the word "Idumaea," so the Idumaeans were descendants of Esau. This is important because, as I have said, Herod was an Idumaean, which means he was an Edomite.

From beginning to end, the Hebrew Scriptures (what Christians call the Old Testament) paint a picture of the Edomites and the Israelites in constant conflict. There are also many prophecies directed against the Edomites because of their harsh treatment of Israel. For instance, in Numbers 24:17 we read about a ruler to be born out of the tribe of Jacob who will ultimately conquer Edom. The entire book of Obadiah is written against the Edomites and predicts the demise of the nation.

Some scholars think that Herod, as an Edomite, would have been aware of these Scriptures and others that prophesy a king coming out of Israel who will conquer the descendants of Esau. Part of Herod's paranoia, then, was the result of his fear that these prophecies were coming true in the birth of Jesus. That was why he insisted on murdering the male children in and around Bethlehem who were near Jesus in age.

This is why he and all of Jerusalem with him were "disturbed" at the announcement of the Magi. The birth of Jesus was a threat to Herod and all he stood for. It exposed Herod as the counterfeit "king of the Jews."

If Luke's account of the Christmas story contrasts two kingdoms, that of Rome and that of God, then Matthew's contrasts two kings, both candidates for the title "King of the Jews": murderous Herod, willing to do anything to stay in power, and the revolutionary Jesus, born amidst straw and dung and worshiped by shepherds and foreigners. No two kings could be more dissimilar.

The Reversal of Everything

The whitewashed, watered-down version of the Christmas story many of us celebrate leads us inevitably to the tame and safe gift shop Jesus. But if we understand his birth as revolution, then we may glimpse the revolution that his life will bring. Jesus has been, and always will be, a threat to the established order of things. This should no longer surprise us today. Two thousand years of church history should suggest that the movement of Jesus is most dangerous when it is opposed. It should not surprise us that some in our culture find an innocuous "Merry Christmas" or bland nativity scene offensive. Our world doesn't want to be reminded of Christ—because he forces us to choose. In our just-do-it, have-it-all kind of world, the revolution of Jesus forces us to choose:

Who is King? Who is Lord? What empire do you serve? What god do you bow down to?

Why do we as the community of Christ react with such vehemence, insecurity, and victimization when the world tries to remove Jesus from the public sphere? We must be reawakened to the fact that the birth and life of Jesus directly opposes the power and authority of this world. He has been and always will be a threat to everything.

Could it be that many of us have lost this aspect of the Christ? It is possible that we see him primarily as ushering in comfort and security for those of us who follow him but that we have missed him as a firebrand radical who so turned the established order upside down that he was murdered to shut him up?

The revolution of Jesus turned everything upside down. While kings were in their palaces and priests in their temples, the God-King was born in a feeding trough. While the religious elite and wealthy slept unaware of the coming of the Christ, this news was announced to shepherds and foreigners. Instead of being born into a well-established and powerful family, Jesus's parents couldn't even stay with Joseph's family in Bethlehem, most likely because of the scandal of her pregnancy before their official marriage.

This is how love invaded our planet. This is how the revolution began. It's unlikely, even absurd. But the last thing it should be is boring or predictable or explainable. This should incite passionate joy or passionate disdain. This is either the greatest thing ever to happen or the most ridiculous idea ever suggested: That God should come among us as one of the "least of these."

Not only did Jesus's birth turn everything upside down, so did his life and what he taught. You must die to live. You must lose to gain. Weakness is strength. Joy exists in the midst of suffering. Power is restraint. Love those who persecute you. Pray for those who hate you. Caesar isn't Lord and Herod isn't King. It is not the strong or the wealthy who will inherit the earth, but the meek. The kingdom of God won't be given to the religious leaders but to the spiritual idiots (the poor in spirit). Mourners, peacemakers, the merciful, and the persecuted can all find blessing in the kingdom of Jesus.

Jesus Christ is the most subversive man ever to have walked the earth. This is revolution.

Two kingdoms war on this earth. One is led by Herods and Caesars; the other by Jesus Christ. One is built on war, oppression, wealth, power, self-interest, and control; the other on love, faith, hope, freedom, grace, compassion, and truth. One demanded sacrifice; the other offered it in our place. The revolution of Jesus, as embodied in the story of his birth, demands our choice between these two kingdoms.

Will we choose the Jesus of Suburbia—the gift shop, swimming pool Jesus who exists to provide us with health, wealth, comfort, and happiness? Or will we press on to find the Jesus of Nazareth, the most dangerous and radical man ever to walk the face of the earth? I want the real thing. I have tried the other. I have worshiped the counterfeits and settled for less than the revolution Jesus brings. I have moved beyond the unbiblical idea that the primary work of Jesus is giving me a ticket to heaven and now understand that he is asking me for everything, to stand with him against all that is unloving and untrue in our world.

I want my children to grow up understanding that life with Jesus is more than just being nice, or trying not to cuss and get drunk because "that is what good Christians do." I want my children to be so compelled by the real Jesus that they are willing to stand with him, giving their lives to his revolution, not in order to be religious but because there is simply no more exhilarating way to live. I want my kids to see my wife and me as revolutionaries who subvert the dominant belief systems and practices of the world, not out of religious obligation but in wholehearted response to the person of Jesus.

The gospel of Christ wasn't just revolution "back then" (two thousand years ago) or isn't just revolution "someday" (in heaven). It is also right now, right where you are, with the people who surround you in your job, your life, your hobby, your home.

Jesus is a threat to everything, for he turns all things upside down. Our job as the community of his followers is neither to add to nor to take away from the offense of Jesus and his message. Far too many of us add to the offense of Jesus, proclaiming his message with meanness and condemnation or gleefully rejoicing over the idea of hell and punishment. But far too many of us make the opposite error as well, softening Jesus to try to tone him down. We apologize for some of his teachings (Did he really tell us to love *everybody*?). We downplay his being the only way to the Father. In so doing, we not only miss the revolution of Jesus for ourselves but also misrepresent him to others.

A Better Way

Jesus never condemned the world without offering an alternative. He stood against evil and sin and the multitude of ways we hurt each other, but he always embodied something better. It wasn't enough simply to condemn wealth (or, more precisely, the worship of it); he would also show the way of simplicity and generosity. It wasn't enough to condemn revenge; he showed us the way of reconciliation and forgiveness. He was countercultural in every sense of the word. Instead of climbing over people to find greatness, serve them. Instead of using people to further your own agenda, give yourself away and you will find true meaning and significance. The power and authority of Jesus lies not just in exposing our sin but also in offering a better way.

My wife and I have been thinking and praying about this for some time now. We have decided to try to live the revolution we've found ourselves in.

We decided to wage war on our neighbors.

We have two different neighbors who are very unfriendly:

a man who lives three doors down and a lady who lives half a block up our street. When we first moved into our home, they didn't wave, smile, or in any way acknowledge our early attempts to be neighborly. The Caesar/Herod impulse in me tells me to love only those who love me. So that's what I did. I don't have time for mean people (unless, of course, I'm the mean person), so I basically ignored them. I wasn't mean, but I wasn't kind either.

Then I started studying and thinking about the revolution. I began to think and pray about what the revolution meant for my neighbors and me. I decided to take this whole "Love thy neighbor" thing seriously. So, as an act of rebellion, I decided to wave, honk, and smile any time I drove by them. (I know this is a silly example.) My decision had nothing to do with getting them to wave back at me, but it had everything to do with how I saw them. Would I be willing to love them even if they weren't loving to me? That was the real issue.

For weeks I did this. I even took my two-year-old over to introduce myself to one of them. (I figured the two-year-old might disarm some of the meanness.) We had a great talk, and my son picked up some new and colorful words. I didn't do anything much, just asked this guy about his life and how long he had lived in the neighborhood. It was amazing just to hear his story.

And the mean lady up the street actually waved back at me three weeks ago. I couldn't believe it.

Who knows if they will come to know Jesus. All I know is

that Jesus wanted me to fight against the Caesar in me and to subvert the dominant paradigms of the world. For me, saying hello and being friendly were part of the revolution.

Again, this is a trivial example of how deep and wide the revolution goes. It encompasses the glorious and the mundane, the superficial and the deepest parts of our souls.

Here is another example. My wife and I recently refinanced our house and cashed out what was (for us) a large sum of money. I spent several weeks dreaming of ways to spend it. It was near Christmas, and I had been studying the birth of Jesus and what it really would have meant to those who heard about it first. As I was praying and prepping for the messages I would teach in the weeks of December, God brought to my mind (as well as to my wife's, though I didn't know it at the time) that revolution for us would be to give away more money than we spent on ourselves this Christmas. With tears of great joy and freedom, my wife and I agreed and then proceeded to ask the dangerous and wonderful question, "Okay, Lord, who's going to get all this money?" We had a blast giving it away and living the revolution of Christmas.

For one junior high school student in our church, revolution meant that he was going to sit with people at lunch who were sitting by themselves. Can you imagine? The Herods and Caesars of junior high are the opinions of the popular and beautiful, and here is a kid who sees Jesus doing much more than giving him a ticket to heaven. How dangerous will this student become if he is free from what others think of him?

A teacher approached me after a service one weekend and told me that revolution for her meant she was going to tell her class the Christmas story, though she had been warned not to. She had glimpsed the subversive, revolutionary Jesus and wanted to join him in his work.

Two thousand years later, no one is singing songs about Herod or giving themselves to the kingdom of Caesar.[7] Herod's kingdom is dust, Rome is ensconced in museums, yet billions gather in the name of Jesus each week. No matter how many Caesars and Herods fill this world, they will never have the last word. The revolution of Jesus will see to that.

2

THE NARROW ROAD

Many of us have done a great disservice to Jesus Christ. Not only do we tone him down to tame and soften him, but we also understand his message to be addressed primarily to *our* needs of comfort, safety, and convenience. We have been telling people that if they come to Jesus, they will live a safe and comfortable life: "He'll be your rock and fortress, and he'll protect you from the dangers around you." Some even insist that Jesus wants nothing more than to heal you, bless you financially, and make your life carefree.

Jesus does heal, of course, and bless us financially and bring peace. But all of that does not even come close to Scripture's teaching on what it means to follow Jesus. If you follow Jesus, you follow the most radical man who ever existed. He marches into the world with kindness, peace, and love, and offers people a whole new way of looking at the world and living within it. His is the most radical message you can preach or live. He turns everything upside down and calls us to do likewise. Jesus is not vitally committed to our comfort and safety; he is committed to the advancing of his kingdom revolution in the hearts of people everywhere.

In talking about what his kingdom is like, Jesus announced, "From the days of John the Baptist until now, the kingdom of heaven has been forcefully advancing, and forceful men take hold of it" (Matt. 11:12). In other words, God is doing something so powerful and dangerous that only those who are willing to embrace it with forceful intensity may take hold of the movement of God's kingdom. The revolution of Jesus isn't for the faint of heart or the middle-of-the-road. It isn't safe. It isn't comfortable. It costs us a great deal to say yes. We take hold of the revolution by abandoning ourselves to Jesus and letting go of everything else.

There is a church in our area that advertises itself with this invitation: "Biblical Principles to Maximize Your Life and Living." I've got nothing against biblical principles or living the way Jesus intended. If we followed biblical principles, we would surely be better off. My beef with this slogan is that it nowhere comes close to the invitation of Jesus. If you are content with your life and comfortable in this world, then I suppose biblical principles will suffice. I guess that's why we have so much teaching and reading of the "three steps to a better marriage, five principles of success" variety. Jesus supposedly makes me a better spouse, child, friend, or coworker. According to this view, he enhances my life.

But for those of us who see the darkness in our souls and the wickedness in our hearts, who feel the desperation and pain of this broken world, biblical principles aren't enough. I don't need enhancement; I need a new heart and a new mind. I need Jesus to invade my life and take it over. I don't want principles or religion or piety; I want him. I'm desperate, I'm empty, and I am not content simply to be my same old self "new and improved"; I want to be something else entirely. I want to lay hold of the movement of Jesus and be turned inside out and upside down. But what I want is costly. Jesus never promises safety and comfort. He promises life with him and a renewed soul, heart, and mind.

I knew someone who was dying of AIDS in the early 1990s from a tainted blood transfusion. He was seventeen when he contracted the disease and died five years later. He came to Christ during that time and spent the remaining years of his life traveling to college campuses sharing his story (this was when AIDS was still relatively unknown) and sharing his faith. I talked with him one evening and was amazed to hear that he praised God for his illness because through it he had found Jesus. I listened to him with an acute ache in my soul as I realized that he had laid hold of the kingdom forcefully and I was still toying around with it.

A young woman I knew of was withering away from multiple sclerosis. She met the disease head on with joy and grace. She would often accompany her husband in a cart while he would play golf. A freak tee shot broke all the bones around one of her eyes and left her in danger of being blind. Her faith and grateful heart were on display as she rode to the hospital and while she was in the emergency room. Because of her witness, two nurses came to faith in Jesus Christ. She was a revolutionary who had grabbed hold of Jesus and refused to let go.

A woman in our church community lost her husband without warning over a year ago, leaving her with two boys on the verge of manhood. Yet I sat listening to her recently as she explained the joy she had felt over the past year—a joy she had previously thought impossible. Another couple in our community went through the pain of finding out the husband had had an affair. They sat with my wife and me one night, recounting the many ways God had restored, renewed, and revealed himself to them in the last three months. Both of them have made hard choices to obey Jesus through forgiveness and repentance, and both see God move greatly in their lives and marriage.

All of these people have two things in common. They saw the power of God in their lives as they laid hold of his kingdom, and they did so through great pain and brokenness. Anyone who tells you that following Jesus will solve all your problems has neither read the whole Bible nor taken time to hear the stories of those who follow Christ.

Erwin McManus points out the flaw in the cliché, The safest place to be is in the center of God's will. "Nonsense," he argues, "The truth of the matter is that the center of

God's will is not a safe place, but the most dangerous place in the world!"[1] I couldn't agree more. Consider the testimony of Paul:

> What anyone else dares to boast about—I am speaking as a fool—I also dare to boast about. Are they Hebrews? So am I. Are they Israelites? So am I. Are they Abraham's descendants? So am I. Are they servants of Christ? (I am out of my mind to talk like this.) I am more. I have worked much harder, been in prison more frequently, been flogged more severely, and been exposed to death again and again. Five times I received from the Jews the forty lashes minus one. Three times I was beaten with rods, once I was stoned, three times I was shipwrecked, I spent a night and a day in the open sea, I have been constantly on the move. I have been in danger from rivers, in danger from bandits, in danger from my own countrymen, in danger from Gentiles; in danger in the city, in danger in the country, in danger at sea; and in danger from false brothers. I have labored and toiled and have often gone without sleep; I have known hunger and thirst and have often gone without food; I have been cold and naked. Besides everything else, I face daily the pressure of my concern for all the churches. (2 Cor. 11:21–28)

This is how Paul describes his life: there is danger everywhere (see 2 Cor. 6:3–10). But it was a danger specific to Paul, a danger that he brought with him everywhere he went. For Paul, being at the center of the will of God was dangerous. And so it is for hundreds of millions of followers of Jesus today. Only in the West has the heretical notion that God will protect us from all harm really taken root. Biblical principles will never lead us into this dangerous life, nor will the Jesus of Suburbia. That is why both are so popular. But neither will ultimately satisfy.

The reason the center of God's will is so dangerous is not simply because our God is a dangerous God who is more interested in forming us and shaping us than he is in making us happy. There is another reason. We are opposed by an enemy far more cunning and powerful than we care to admit. We all agree that Jesus defeated the powers of darkness on the cross, yet many of us remain woefully naïve to the fact that our adversary continues to war against God's purposes and people, even in defeat. I know the subject of spiritual warfare is either obsessed over (so that everything is the result of demonic attack) or ignored completely (so that nothing is), but the reality for those who have decided to follow Jesus is that they have put on a bull's-eye and become targets of the enemy. We don't tell people this when we are asking them to consider Jesus, but we should. To say yes to Christ is to enter actively into the war that rages around us while most of the world remains blissfully unaware. To follow Jesus is to choose a side decisively and to place oneself squarely in the enemy's sights.

War isn't just one picture the Bible gives us about our lives but instead serves as the backdrop for everything else. Peter tells us, "Your enemy the devil prowls around like a roaring lion looking for someone to devour" (1 Pet. 5:8). Paul also reminds us that "our struggle is not against flesh and blood, but against the rulers, against the authorities, against the powers of this dark world and against the spiritual forces of evil in the heavenly realm" (Eph. 6:12). Many of us know these verses but simply do not live like we believe them. Jesus waged war during his ministry. He cast out demons, rebuked illness, went about binding the strongman (a reference to Satan), and confronted evil and death wherever he found it. He gave his followers the same authority, knowing they would need it in the battles they would fight. In fact, John announces that "the reason the Son of God appeared was to destroy the devil's work" (1 John 3:8).

The second part of John 10:10 is well known: "I have come that they may have life, and have it to the full." But it is interesting to me that we very rarely mention the first part of the verse, "The thief comes only to steal and kill and destroy." We all want the life that Jesus has for us, but few of us are willing to fight for it.[2] Do we really believe that Satan kills, steals, and destroys? Do we believe he devours?

We must learn to live in this reality. Not to fear it, but rather to be aware of it. Stepping out in obedience to Jesus is dangerous on two counts. First, Jesus is wild and radical and will lead us to places we would probably not go otherwise (though they will always be worth it). Second, we place ourselves in the middle of the great conflict that has raged against God's people for centuries. We must call this situation what it is. Until we do that, we will not be able to make sense of much of what happens to us. Many have believed or hoped that becoming a follower of Jesus would somehow end their troubles, never knowing that they were instead going to the front lines of the fiercest battle of their lives.

If we understood this, we might be better able to see Jesus in the midst of the evil that threatens the world. When Allied soldiers invaded Normandy on D-Day, none of them were surprised to find themselves being shot at. Nobody was shocked that there was blood in the water or that there were casualties in the battle. But when we accept the reality of the spiritual world and the forces within it—good *and* evil—then we cease being surprised that marriages blow out or that children rebel or that bad things do happen to good people (sometimes precisely *because* they are good). We will be aware of the temptations, the subtle or overt accusations, or the deceptions that are set against the children of God with staggering effectiveness.

Take prayer, for instance. Unanswered prayer confounds many of us. We fall into the trap of thinking that God is not good or not interested in our lives and requests. But an episode in the book of Daniel paints a different picture. Daniel received a vision that he did not understand, so he asked God to make its meaning plain to him. For three weeks Daniel waited for an answer, "I, Daniel, mourned for three weeks. I ate no choice food; no meat or wine touched my lips; and I used no lotions at all until the three weeks were over" (Dan. 10:2–3). At the end of that time, an angel appeared to Daniel with this message, "Since the first day that you set your mind to gain understanding and to humble yourself before your God, your words were heard, and I have come in response to them. But the prince of the Persian kingdom resisted me twenty-one days. Then Michael, one of the chief princes, came to help me, because I was detained there with the king of Persia" (Dan. 10:12–13).

In other words, Daniel waited three weeks for an answer to his prayer because the angel sent to answer Daniel was opposed for that time by demonic forces. Now I am not suggesting this is always the reason behind our (seemingly) unanswered prayers, but it does place prayer into the larger conflict in which we find ourselves.

The point is that we do not do justice to what it means to follow Jesus Christ. His revolution demands our complete surrender to him, and our obedience doesn't guarantee a problem-free life. In fact, it may lead to just the opposite. We must be very clear about this, for Jesus asked his followers again and again to count the cost of following him. If we did the same thing, invited people to consider what it really means to follow Jesus, then perhaps our churches would have fewer consumers and more disciples.

A Word about God's Will

Next to the classic question "How far can I go with someone of the opposite sex before marriage?" questions about knowing the will of God are the most common I receive (and have asked, myself). It seems there are many of us who have decided to take hold of God's kingdom forcefully and do something great for his name, only to be paralyzed by the idea that we step outside God's will if we are not careful. Many passionate, gifted followers of Jesus don't do much because they are waiting for the planets to align or for God to write something on the wall!

Much of the debate around God's will makes it a bigger deal than do the Scriptures. The scriptural teaching on the will of God that has set me free is this: God will guide those whose hearts are open to follow. It is that simple. Be faithful in what God calls you to today, and he will lead you tomorrow. God is more committed to having you walk in his will than you are.[3] If you have a heart that is passionately trying to do God's will, he will lead you.

Pharaohs stood against God and failed; Nazis and communists have tried to stamp out God's movement and succeeded only in spreading it farther; Caesars and Herods have shaken their fists at God, but no one has ever been able to stop the purposes of God in human history. Why, then, if we believe God to be that powerful, do we think we can so easily miss doing his will? God is so good, so sovereign, and so caring that he will reveal his will to us if our hearts are open. There are no magic formulas to this, no seven-step lists to memorize, no guaranteed incantations. There is just the simple trust that God will lead us where he wants us to go and we cannot miss it if we simply keep our eyes open.

If anyone was "in good" with God, it was the apostle Paul. Paul wrote over half of the New Testament and founded countless churches. You would think he would know the secret of finding and following God's will. Acts 16 records for us an amusing story:

> Paul and his companions traveled throughout the region of Phrygia and Galatia, having been kept by the Holy Spirit from preaching the word in the province of Asia. When they came to the border of Mysia, they tried to enter Bithynia, but the Spirit of Jesus would not allow them to. So they passed by Mysia and went down to Troas. During the night Paul had a vision of a man of Macedonia standing and begging him, "Come over to Macedonia and help us." After Paul had seen the vision, we got ready at once to leave for Macedonia, concluding that God had called us to preach the gospel to them. (vv. 6–10)

This is almost comical. Paul and his friends are stopped by God two different times from going to the wrong place. Paul evidently had no idea where to go; he just knew he was supposed to go somewhere. He had enough faith that God would redirect him if he were headed in the wrong direction. God finally had to speak so simply to Paul in a dream that there was no possible way he could misunderstand. God simply would not let Paul go elsewhere.

We know enough of God's will from the Scriptures to be busy enough. Today I am called to be a faithful husband, a loving father, a diligent pastor, a courageous witness, a prayerful worshiper, a law-abiding citizen, and an appreciative son. That is plenty. I have no idea where I will be five years from now, and I have ceased caring. I am going to be faithful in what God has called me to do today, knowing that tomorrow he will direct me.

If you passionately commit yourself to living out his purposes and advancing his kingdom, then God will make sure you live in his will. Trust him that if you are not going in the right direction, he will redirect you. But, I urge you, if you are paralyzed by the idea of the will of God, do *something*. Doing anything God-honoring is far better than doing nothing at all. And you'll be amazed at what God does when you step out in obedience to what you already know to do.

There have been times when I have received very specific guidance on where to go or what to do (or even what to say). It has been my observation that God's will for us rarely makes sense to us looking forward, but it almost always makes sense in retrospect. God has led me to move across the country to marry a woman who ended up breaking my heart. He did this to help make me ready for the one *he* had for me.

He led me out of the business world because I was a slave to money. He has led me to churches at which I would never have imagined working, to do things I never thought I was capable of doing. All the while he was inviting me deeper and deeper into his revolution, asking me to hold onto him with greater intensity and purpose. As C. S. Lewis has said, Jesus isn't safe, but he is good.

The Gospel of Risk Management

What keeps us from a life of such faith is that we have become very good at assessing and minimizing risk. Our culture is all about risk management. We want to hedge our finances against future market downturns, and we have home insurance, life insurance, car insurance, fire insurance, flood insurance, and earthquake insurance. Athletes and entertainers can insure parts of their bodies against injury. We sign prenuptial agreements to protect us from the financial ramifications of divorce, and we have health plans to protect us when we are sick. We practice birth control and watch our blood pressure. We wear seat belts and helmets. I see the need for most of these things, but we have become people who focus on managing and minimizing risk everywhere we see it. We love the illusion of danger but not the real thing. I can ride a roller coaster and *feel* out of control, while remaining safely buckled into my seat.

We want Jesus to be the same way: all reward, no risk. We

don't give ourselves fully to him because we are afraid he will send us to China or ask us to become poor. We want the illusion of faith, as long as we are safe. But walking with God is not a no-risk proposition; it is one of the most dangerous things you can do. Risk is inherent in the life of faith. Risk and faith cannot be divorced.

This is one of the reasons we settle for the mundane Jesus of Suburbia; he is predictable and safe. This way of living steals the life God offers, even with all of its costs. We settle for the dull and drab, never daring great things for God and never seeing God do great things.

We are seldom afraid of opposition that is much smaller than we are. When we keep our challenges manageable, we not only manage our fear of risk but also squelch our faith. We may look courageous when all we have done is minimize our risk. When God calls us to something, his call invokes both faith and fear. It should. God always summons us to something bigger than ourselves. He loves waiting until all other hope has failed and our natural, human resources are exhausted. Then he shows up and turns the tide. When he calls us to battle, the opposition will always be greater than the strength we have. When the odds are in our favor, we may be tempted to give the credit to ourselves. God wants whatever happens in our lives to be unexplainable apart from him. Paul says this in 2 Corinthians 4:7: "But we have this treasure in jars of clay to show that this all-surpassing power is from God and not from us."

This is why God allowed the Israelites to be trapped

between the Red Sea and the Egyptian army. This is why he asked Gideon, the weakest member of the weakest tribe, to whittle his army down from thirty thousand to three hundred so that God could receive the glory. This is why God sometimes allows us to get in so far over our heads that only he can save us. We are promised victory, not tranquility.

We have a part to play in this life of risk and faith. Jesus calls us beyond our comfort level to step into obedience and watch God do great and mighty things. We say to God, "Show me and I'll believe." Instead, God says to us, "Believe, and I'll show you." This is the life of following Jesus Christ. We say, "God, show me your will and I'll obey you." God says, "Obey me, and I'll show you my will." God isn't looking for a bunch of "I should do this because that's what good Christians do" kind of people. He is looking for "I wouldn't miss this for the world" kind of people.

The Invitation

So what is the gospel? It certainly is the good news about Jesus reconciling everything to God through his sacrifice. It certainly is the joy of being forgiven and receiving a new identity as a son or daughter of God. It certainly means spending forever in God's presence and seeing Jesus face to face.

But it most certainly does not mean a life without risk or danger. The life of faith solves many problems but introduces new (and often more difficult) ones. It answers many questions but leads to many more. It forces us to trust the wild and dangerous God who cannot be boxed into our theologies, language, or experience. Far too many new followers of Jesus have had their faith shipwrecked because they were sold the lie that life with Jesus is trouble free. Far too many of us have wrapped our message around the idolatrous promise that Jesus will bring safety and security.

The kingdom of Jesus is forcefully advancing. Jesus told us that he did not come to bring peace, but division (Luke 12:51–53). He promised that in this world we will have trouble (John 16:33). We should not be surprised at suffering or persecution (1 Pet. 4:12–19; 2 Tim. 3:12). The center of God's will is the most dangerous place to be. We each have to decide whether our lives will be risk free and safe or faith filled and dangerous.

This, too, is the invitation of Jesus: to abandon ourselves to him with no hope that we'll be able to control or manage him. He will sustain us; the victory is ours because it is his, and yet the battle still rages. We must fight for the life he offers. Jesus doesn't want a blind, naïve commitment from followers who expect only blessings. He was quite clear about the costs of following him. My request is that we be just as faithful.

Often, at the highest points of his favor with the crowds, Jesus would remind people of the cost of being his follower:

> If anyone comes to me and does not hate his father and mother, his wife and his children, his brothers and sisters—

yes, even his own life—he cannot be my disciple. And anyone who does not carry his cross and follow me cannot be my disciple. Suppose one of you wants to build a tower. Will he not first sit down and estimate the cost to see if he has enough money to complete it? For if he lays the foundation and is not able to finish it, everyone who sees it will ridicule him, saying, "This fellow began to build and was not able to finish." Or suppose a king is about to go to war against another king. Will he not first sit down and consider whether he is able with ten thousand men to oppose the one coming against him with twenty thousand? If he is not able, he will send a delegation while the other is still a long way off and will ask for terms of peace. In the same way, any of you who does not give up everything he has cannot be my disciple. (Luke 14:26–33)

How many times have we heard *this* invitation at an evangelistic crusade? My question is this: Have we turned the ruthless and demanding invitation of Jesus of Nazareth into a safe and weak invitation to follow the counterfeit Jesus of Suburbia? Jesus consistently and frequently warned his followers about the cost of being his disciple. Why don't we do the same thing today?

3

THE FAILURE OF RELIGION

These days, if somebody asks me if I am religious, I usually say no. The words *religion* and *religious* have taken on such negative baggage that I am not sure what someone means by those words when they ask. The same thing seems to be true for the word *Christian*. If someone asks me if I am a Christian, I don't know how to answer because I am no longer sure what it means to be one. I love Jesus; I have committed my life to him in service, obedience, and worship; and I love his church. But I am not sure we know any longer what it means to be a Christian. For some, to be Christian is to simply be American: we are a "Christian" nation, we are told. For others, to be Christian is to be raised in the church—maybe attending only at Easter and Christmas—but holding on to some vague sense of "how I was raised." Still others claim to be Christian on the sole basis of a prayer they prayed as a young child.

I was raised in Sunday school, learning about a nice, tame Jesus from flannel graph stories and from well-meaning teachers. I found him boring and irrelevant to how I actually lived. This continued into high school, when Jesus became my spiritual 9-1-1 hotline and church was where I went to meet girls. I lived all this time without the slightest idea of what it really meant to follow Jesus Christ. I had prayed to invite Jesus into my life (whatever that meant) because, given the choice between praying to Jesus or frying in hell, I figured praying was the better deal.

After praying that prayer, I learned there was a whole bunch of stuff I now had to start doing. I needed to have a "quiet time" with God every morning, go to church, give money to the church, pray, share my faith, and avoid the "big" sins. I was taught that Christians don't listen to "secular" music, don't attend parties, don't make out with girls, and don't smoke or drink or cuss. This was how I understood "following Jesus": do the good things and avoid the bad things. I knew I was saved by grace, but once I became a follower of Jesus, I thought grace no longer applied. I thought it became my job to become a better person.

This all seemed pretty straightforward. It's what I expected from "religion." As I began to try to live this way, I realized one of the perks of this approach to God was that I could know how I was doing. All I had to do was to check my list of good things to do and bad things to avoid. If my good score was better than my bad score, then Jesus was pleased. I not only kept score for myself but soon realized I could keep score for others, too. I could apply the same list to them. And no matter how bad I was, I could always find someone worse. (I could always find someone better, too, but that never seemed to be my focus.)

I tried being a Christian this way for a long time, but the more I tried to be "good," the more I failed; and the more I wanted to avoid bad things, the more they became attractive. Not only that, but keeping score was exhausting! I never knew if God was really pleased with me; it just seemed that God was more interested in keeping me from having fun than he was about anything else.

This was my experience with Christianity, the organized religion. I learned a lot, and I tried to be a good person. I knew about God's love and grace, but that knowledge never set me free from perpetual striving and the sense that God wasn't pleased with me because I wasn't trying hard enough.

I became a youth pastor, went to seminary, and became very good at teaching people to follow Jesus this way. But everything changed at a retreat in 2000. The speaker was Bart Tarman, then the chaplain at Westmont College. The focus of the whole weekend was Jesus—not Christianity, but Jesus. He talked about how Jesus loved people and how Jesus engaged the culture around him. He talked about how Jesus hated empty religion and loved to see expressions of simple faith in him. For the first time in my life, I realized I hadn't been given the whole story about Jesus. He was much more interesting than I had been led to believe. I realized I had not really been following Jesus; I had been a follower of Christianity—an organized set of rules and beliefs substituted in his place. I finally moved on from the gift shop Jesus and glimpsed the real thing.

That weekend changed everything; it became my defining moment. It changed how I taught, how I pastored, how I loved my wife, how I saw my job, and how I viewed people who were not into Jesus. Everything changed. I began to understand what "following Jesus" really meant. So I committed my life to Jesus again that weekend—not only as the forgiver of my sins but also as someone I wanted to learn to love. He became someone I wanted to hang out with and learn from, someone who showed me a vision of this life that made me hunger and thirst for more of him. I had been a Christian most of my life but had not, until that point, understood how radical he was.

The Danger of Religion

I began to read the Gospels differently. I noticed that the Pharisees of the Gospels—whom Jesus criticized most severely—were also incredibly religious. They took the 610 laws of the Hebrew Scriptures and added more than 1,500 other rules. Philip Yancey, in his book *The Jesus I Never Knew*, does a great job of helping us see their devotion to Jewish Law.[1] They prayed, fasted, tithed, sought converts, taught "Saturday school" in the synagogues, and memorized and studied Scripture. They went to unbelievable extremes to keep the commandments of God, and yet Jesus saved his harshest criticism for them. He called them snakes and white-washed tombs, hypocrites and blind guides. He told them that hookers were getting into the kingdom of heaven ahead of them. It is difficult to overstate how offensive and critical Jesus was about their whole approach to following God. He loved them, of course, and many came to faith in him. But he always condemned their attempts to justify themselves through their religious performance, even going so far as to observe that often-empty religion is more spiritually dangerous than outright immorality (Matt. 21:28–31).

As I began to observe the practices of the Pharisees and Jesus's response to them, I saw that the Pharisees' approach to God was the same approach I had been taught years ear-lier: learn to keep score, do good things and avoid bad things, focus on what you can see others do and on what others can see you do. In fact, it struck me as incredibly inconsistent that the Pharisees were often portrayed as the "bad guys" of the Gospels when their approach to spirituality was no different than that of many Christians I knew.

Here's the crazy thing: Jesus told the Pharisees they were missing him *because* of their religiousness. Religion got in the way of finding and following Jesus Christ. They were so focused on doing the right things and avoiding the wrong things, keeping score and pronouncing judgment on others, that they missed Jesus entirely. In fact, they did more than miss him; some of them went so far as to accuse Jesus of being a front man for Satan, rather than acknowledge him as Messiah.

Jesus makes a similar point in the parable of the prodigal son. We tend to think that the lost, younger son is the point of the parable. But because Jesus was speaking to Pharisees and teachers of Jewish law when he told this story, I suspect that the older, obedient son is the focus. The older son's resentment toward his father's treatment of his lost and broken brother was a mirror for the Pharisees to see their treatment of the "sinners" around them and their resentment toward Jesus. It was precisely the older son's *obedience* (and his pride, judgment, and sense of entitlement because of it) that kept him from being part of his younger brother's welcome and restoration into the family.

And that is the danger: religion can convince us we are "good" when in fact we, like the younger brother, need the father's restoration and forgiveness (see the parable of the Pharisee and the tax collector in Luke 18). In the end, we see that both sons were lost, the younger to immorality and irreligiousness and the older to grudging obedience and self-righteousness. But it is the older brother who ends up missing the party. The warning is powerful: "The elder brother is not lost *despite* his obedience to the father but *because* of it."[2]

Revolution or Religion?

When I use the term *religion* (or *religious*), I want to be clear what I mean. By "religion," I mean any system of rules and rituals designed to bring us into relationship with God. It is the idea that somehow we can win God's blessing through our efforts to do good and avoid bad.

One of the words we see in the New Testament that is translated to mean "religion" is *threskeia*, which refers to the external aspects of someone's internal beliefs. *Threskeia* refers to the outward trappings that may (or may not) be associated with genuine faith. It is primarily the ceremonial aspect of religious behavior. This is how the word is mainly used today. When most people speak of being religious or having found religion, they are referring to some of the rituals, rules, and traditions that too easily take the place of a genuine relationship with God. Someone is considered religious if they read their holy book, say their prayers, and do good deeds for the less fortunate. This kind of religiousness comes in all shapes and sizes, and is the enemy of what Jesus came to give us.[3]

We must be equally careful to avoid the opposite danger. I am not suggesting that the church abandon its rituals or calls to holy living. Actions, practices, and resources that are sometimes part of pursuing genuine faith are not bad things in themselves. In fact, I believe genuine faith leads to changes in outward behavior (as we'll see in the next chapter). But when the externals become substitutes for the real thing—an authentic relationship with God—they have fallen to the level of empty religion. This approach to God, Jesus suggested, misses God entirely.

What a sobering thought: the ones most opposed to the work of Jesus were the most devoutly religious. Could such a thing happen today? I think it can and does. Empty religion, even disguised as "Christian," is a stumbling block for many to come to faith. Those outside the church either obey the rules (and decide they are good people who do not really need saving) or give up trying altogether.

Jesus offers a radically different view of life with God. He founded a revolution, a radical invasion of the kingdom of heaven and shalom into the kingdoms of the earth.[4] It was never meant to be codified and systematized into organized religion. Christianity, if it is really of Jesus, is not one of the world's great religions. It is not a religion at all. It is something else entirely.

Jesus came to abolish religion. If this is true, then why did God give all sorts of rules and instructions (over six hundred of them!) to his people in the Old Testament? And why did Jesus say he was fulfilling the law and not abolishing it (Matt. 5:20)? Wasn't God establishing a religion (in our sense of the word) when he gave his people the Ten Commandments?

No, he was not. The Ten Commandments (like the rest of the Old Testament law) were given to a people *already redeemed*. God rescued his people from Egypt as an act of grace (he was quite clear that they had nothing to do with their redemption) and *then* showed them how to live as a redeemed people. God set them free and then told them how to stay that way. The Old Testament, just like the New Testament, is the story of grace. God calls his people out of slavery then beckons them to live out what they have already received. That's why James calls the Old Testament "the perfect law that gives freedom" (James 1:25).

Even the sacrifices of the Old Testament point to the grace of Jesus. Rules and rituals are given to God's people to remind them what God is like and what he's called them to. God's commands are for our good, but they (by themselves) do not make us right with him.

The problem was that, in Jesus's day (seemingly much like our own), people had turned rules and regulations into ends in and of themselves: they became the focus, and the relationship God intended between his people and himself was lost. Jesus came to do away with the meaningless ritual and empty religion of the day and to call people into relationship with himself. He came to turn us not into religious people but into joyful and holy people, abandoned to him so as to do his work on earth. He came to turn us into people who know how to love and celebrate.

Where Jesus was, joy was. You don't tear the roof off a house to lower your friend in front of someone who is joyless. You don't drop everything to follow someone who is not joyful. You don't fight through crowds, hoping just to touch the hem of his robe, if he is not full of joy. He was not (and still is not) impressed with joyless religiosity (Luke 18:9–14). So he calls both "younger sons" and "older brothers" to come to joyful faith in him.

How the revolution of Jesus differs from empty religion is seen when we look at two of Jesus's objections to empty religion.

Consider the Fruit Tree

One of Jesus's most perplexing statements is found in Matthew 5:20: "For I tell you that unless your righteousness surpasses that of the Pharisees and the teachers of the law, you will certainly not enter the kingdom of heaven." As we have pointed out, the Pharisees and scribes were masters at maintaining strict adherence to Jewish law and tradition. Those who heard Jesus's words must have been astonished to hear Jesus say this. What was he saying? If the Pharisees obeyed 2,100 commands and rules, must we obey 2,101 in order to please God?

Jesus goes on to explain that God is not looking for "more and more" obedience but "deeper and deeper" obedience.[5] True obedience is of the heart. Externals matter only to the degree that they reflect (and affect) the heart. The Pharisees were content with rigid, formal obedience and conformity to the letter of the Law. Jesus teaches us that God's demands are far more radical: he is concerned with what is going on in our hearts and minds. Jesus deepens God's requirements of us in order to have a relationship with him, shattering the religious myth that we can somehow be good enough to earn his favor.

The religious people of Jesus's day made external behavior the focus. But Jesus pointed out that while religiousness can make a good show of devotion, it cannot develop the real thing. We can act lovingly, of course, but does that mean we really love? We can avoid major sexual sin, but does this mean we are sexually pure? Jesus's answer to both questions is no. It is the heart that is the issue, not religious behavior.

So Jesus didn't come to change our behavior; he came to change our hearts. Religion—emphasizing and focusing on changing our behavior—will never touch the darkness in our hearts. Jesus comes not espousing another religious approach to God but rather preaching the invasion of God's kingdom—*right where we are*. We don't have to get "cleaned up" first. As we receive God's grace and the rule of God's kingdom *in* us, Jesus works to change our hearts into hearts that naturally do the things that God requires.

If you have a Bible available, read the rest of Matthew 5. Jesus gives six examples of how the religious leaders actually lessened God's commands by restricting their application to outward behavior only. To Pharisees who boasted about their sexual purity (in obedience to the command not to commit adultery), Jesus speaks of the heart issue of lust, the place where adultery is born. Instead of just talking about murder, Jesus goes to the heart issue of anger, where the impulse to murder begins.

Jesus's point in each example is the same. Religion can restrain behavior, but it cannot change the human heart. And the heart is what makes us clean or unclean (Mark 7:14–23). The most important commands of God don't have to do with praying a certain number of times per day or giving a certain amount of money to the poor. Jesus's summary of the whole law is simply this: love God and love each other.

Focusing on externals will never make that happen. Religion can help us act lovingly, but it can't turn us into loving people. Only the power of God can do that. The real test of spiritual maturity is not how much we read our Bible or how many people we lead to Christ; it is how well we love. And this is the rub: some of us, if all we were called to was an outward show of loving behavior, might be able to get away with it. But to be turned into people who really give out of love, serve out of love, submit out of love, speak out of love, and obey out of love—who among us can claim complacency when compared to that standard?

I have orange trees in my backyard at home. Turning them into apple trees requires something far greater than merely tying apples to their branches. I could change the appearance of the orange tree by tying apples onto its branches, but no matter how many apples are tied on, the tree will still produce only oranges, as it is designed to do. If I want to change the fruit, I must change the inner nature (in essence, the "heart") of the tree.

Jesus's first criticism of religion is that all the religious activity in the world cannot change what makes us fallen in the first place. While the Pharisees focused on tying religious deeds to their bodies, they were unconcerned with the heart from which true faith flows. Jesus pointed toward the transformation of the heart as the basis of life in his kingdom—something that empty religion and ritual leave untouched.

Olan Mills™ Spirituality

Jesus discussed another problem with empty religion. In Matthew 6:1, Jesus warns against doing our "acts of righteousness" (good deeds) to impress others. He is not teaching that we should hide our good deeds. While that may be appropriate in some cases, it is not Jesus's point here. There is nothing inherently wrong with a good deed being seen. The problem comes when we are doing a good deed *in order* to be seen.

Jesus refers to the people who do religious stuff for show as "hypocrites." The word comes from Greek drama and refers to an actor; the word literally means "one who wears a mask." In Greek plays, the actors would wear masks to convey the emotion of the scene. They would rarely show their real faces. Jesus uses this image to point out that we can use religion in the same way. We can wear a religious mask and actually try to hide from God and others. As long as we do and say the right religious things, we don't have to reveal our true selves.

Jesus gives three examples of the way some used religious

THE JESUS OF SUBURBIA

activities to promote false impressions of themselves. They would wear religious "masks" of behaviors and attitudes in public in order to be seen as pious and devout. Some would announce their giving with great pomp and ceremony, some would pray long and loud on street corners, and some would alter their appearance to make it obvious that they were fasting. In each case, Jesus simply says, if you would rather have the approval of men over the approval of God, so be it. You "have received [your] reward in full" (Matt. 6:2; cf. vv. 5, 16).

If we took a close look, we might find that many of our church and religious activities are structured around actually *evading* God. Rather than really coming before him acknowledging my sinfulness and dependence, it is easier and more satisfying to come before him with a bunch of religious talk and activity. Much like the Pharisee in Luke 18, we think all of our giving, serving, reading, and praying amounts to much in God's eyes. What would church look like if we were really honest about the lust, depression, greed, addiction, slander, deceit, anger, or [fill in the blank] of our lives? What if we quit hiding behind our religious masks and really dealt with the ugliness of our lives before God and others?

When I was growing up, my family went periodically to an Olan Mills™ photography studio to get pictures taken. The very name of the place still strikes fear and anxiety in my heart. I've got nothing against the studio itself. It's just that I dreaded what would happen when we got there. I hated having family pictures taken. We would spend the day of our

appointment arguing like crazy: *Why do we have to do this?*
Why do we have to get dressed up? Nobody is going to care
about these pictures except you, anyway! Why do we have to
all look the same? (I still tense up thinking about it.) We
would argue in the house, during the car ride over, and in the
sitting room waiting for our turn. But then, magically, we
would sit before the camera and pretend we were happy to be
there! We would smile and say "cheese" and do our best to
convey the impression that we were delighted to be together
at that moment. Of course, we would then fight all the way
home about how horrible the whole experience was, but looking at the pictures, you would never have known. We literally
put our "smiling" masks on for the sake of how we appeared.

I wonder how much of what we do at church is like going
to Olan Mills™. We may fight on the way over, have drunk
too much last night, or swear at others under our breath as we
park in the lot, but once we come in, we sing the right songs
and say "Amen" in the right places. And the whole time we
don't have to be honest with God; we can just mouth the right
words and do the right things. We don't have to be honest
with others, either; we can just act the right way and say the
right religious things, and nobody will ask us any questions.

It seems like we spend a lot of time in church avoiding the
messiness and filth of our real lives. We talk about things that
are nice and hopeful but don't address the questions we really
wonder about. We talk about whether the service was "good"
or not, but rarely (it seems) do we care to ask Jesus what he

thought of it. I wonder how much of what we do when we are gathered together is designed to impress and hide instead of to draw us deeper into honest and raw relationship with God and others. We have little time for real openness because we fear it. It may lead to confrontation or make someone uncomfortable. Or people might see us as different than the image we have worked hard to create and sustain. But regardless of its source, the result is the same: "I tell you the truth, they have received their reward" begins to apply to us (Matt. 6:2).

Genuine faith is authentic; it doesn't allow us to hide. The people who saw Jesus for who he was could not help crying out to him in their need (Luke 18:35–43). They were not self-sufficient and independent. Jesus is not for the people who have it all together, the people who are "Fine, thank you" and don't need a thing. Jesus Christ is for those who are tired, weary of religious obligation, sick of themselves, and sick of trying (and failing) to live a good life.

There is a difference between being religious and following Jesus. We can allow our religiousness to get in the way of truly knowing Jesus (as opposed to just knowing *about* him). The cure for this, I think, is to get a glimpse of Jesus. He often goes unrecognized and unknown, even in the church. But those who get a glimpse of the real thing will never settle for a substitute. Those who catch a glimpse of Jesus will never settle again for simply being religious. One glimpse of him as he really is, and you would be a fool not to drop everything and follow him.

So where can we find him? I am amazed at how few people read the Gospels. I guess we think we have read them all before. We went to Sunday school, but did we hear *all* the stories or see Jesus for who he is? It seems like the Jesus of our growing up years is always white and tall and smiling. Have you ever seen a flannel-graph Jesus with a whip—when he got angry right in the middle of church? We like to think of Jesus as being like Mr. Rogers. The problem is, no one would crucify Mr. Rogers.

Jesus got mad at people like us. Jesus was not religious. The people who knew him didn't think of him as a religious person; they thought of him as a radical. It was the religious people who nailed his hands to the cross because he was turning their religious world upside down, and he has done the same thing ever since.

Wherever people glimpsed the real face of Jesus or caught the faintest glimmer of his real feelings or thought a single thought that was like his—wherever that happened, in whatever century, in whatever culture—tremendous change broke out. Revolutions began.

4

THE SCANDAL OF GRACE

There is simply no way I would ever go back to junior high school. Never. I hated junior high. I was physically and socially awkward (OK, not much has changed), and I didn't fit in anywhere. I particularly loathed the time after lunch when we would go out to the playground and pick teams to play kickball or whatever. Tall but uncoordinated, I was usually one of the last ones picked. I *hated* that feeling. I still do. Throughout my childhood, I remember the joy of being picked and included and the embarrassment of being left out. I am pretty sure this is a common human sentiment. Who will invite me to the prom? If I ask her, will she say yes? Will I be picked to make the team? Will I be invited to the party?

This seems to be universal stuff—even for adults! We can all relate to the joy of being chosen and the pain of being excluded. For me, the playground was where this took place every day, but we see it everywhere.

The revolution of Jesus contained many aspects: bringing life where there was death, light where there was darkness, and righteousness where there had been sin. But the single most revolutionary feature of his revolution was the scandal of grace. Where there had been condemnation, Jesus brought grace and forgiveness. This, I believe, was one of the major reasons he was killed. The rulers of the day simply couldn't tolerate some itinerant preacher marching around the Judean countryside healing people of their diseases and forgiving people of their sins. "Proper" messiahs were not expected to behave this way. The coming king was supposed to overthrow the Romans and restore Israel, not welcome outcasts, misfits, and sinners into God's kingdom solely by virtue of his authority.

In the religious context of Jesus's day, exclusion was the rule. God had chosen Israel to be his people—set apart for him and called to put him on display to the world around them. But far too often Israel succumbed to arrogance and separation. Gentiles (people who were not Jewish) were, for the most part, not welcomed into the Jewish community of faith; instead they were called "dogs" and "godless barbarians." Women, made equally in the image of God, were considered second-class citizens (even if they were Jewish) and unworthy of theological training. Much of what God had set up in order to lead the Jewish people to himself and to his grace (and, by extension, leading the others who were watching Israel) had turned into heartless religion.

Let's look at two examples. In each, the Jews had taken something God had designed to be a picture of grace and turned it into a picture of exclusion and hierarchy. These will set the stage for the revolution of Jesus and the scandal of his grace.

The Temple

The first example is the layout of the Jewish temple. In the Old Testament, God gave us pictures of himself and his holiness in the way he instructed Solomon to design the temple. By the time of Jesus, however, Solomon's temple had been destroyed for many years, and King Herod's temple stood in its place. Herod's temple was made up of several courts, each separated by distance and architecture.[1]

The outer court was called the Court of Gentiles and was not considered part of the temple proper (see Acts 21:28). It was the court farthest away from the center of the temple. Gentiles were not allowed to come into the temple and offer sacrifices.

Once inside the temple area, the outermost court was the Court of Women. If you were a Jewish woman, you could come into that court and offer a sacrifice, but you could go no farther. Toward the center of the temple was the Court of Israel, where Jewish men would offer sacrifices. They could go farther than the Jewish women into the temple but were not allowed any farther than the Court of Israel.

Next was the Holy Place. This was the Court of Priests,

where the descendants of Aaron would offer the sacrifices of the people. To be allowed into this court, one had to be Jewish, male, and from the right family line.

Beyond the Holy Place, separated by a foot-thick curtain, was the Most Holy Place—the Holy of Holies. This is where the ark of the covenant was placed and where God himself dwelt among his people. Only the high priest, on the Day of Atonement, could enter to offer sacrifices for the entire nation.

We know God had reasons for designing the temple this way. But I think it is no stretch for us to see how quickly human minds could turn the layout of the temple into a hierarchy of self-righteousness and self-importance. And that is what happened in Jesus's day. The temple, the place where God showed his people mercy as they offered him their sacrifices, became like the junior high playground—a place of hierarchy and exclusion. Instead of welcoming Gentiles into the world of the one true God, the Jews of Jesus's day despised them and turned the Court of Gentiles into a Jews-only marketplace (see John 2:12–25).

Women, likewise, were treated as second-class citizens. They were considered so untrustworthy that their testimony would carry little or no weight in a court of law. (Though I find it interesting that Jesus taught them theology and relied on their testimony as the first eyewitnesses to his resurrection.) Instead of being viewed as equal image bearers of God, women were viewed as property and excluded from many religious activities.

The temple system came to represent the Jews' perception of God's favor: to be considered blessed, you had to be Jewish, male, and rich (or a member of the priesthood). We even have records of Jewish men who would begin their days by thanking God that they weren't a Gentile, a woman, or a slave (see what Paul does with this in Gal. 3:28).

Clean and Unclean

The Jews not only divided the world into Jew and Gentile but also, even within Jewish culture, divided themselves into Jews who were ceremonially clean (fit to go to the temple and offer sacrifice) and those who were ceremonially unclean. This is the second example of how grace became exclusion. In the Old Testament, God gave his people ritual cleanliness laws as another picture of his holiness. Having a certain skin disease or bodily discharge could cause someone to be unclean. He or she would not be allowed to enter the temple area to offer sacrifice until he or she was purified. Many such laws were given to the Jewish people, but God always provided remedies so that those who were unclean could be made clean.

Again, sinful human minds took labels that applied to whether or not someone was ceremonially fit to offer sacrifice and applied them to people as a whole. Instead of recognizing someone as *ritually* unclean (understanding their uncleanliness in terms of being able to go to the temple), Jews began to regard other Jews as simply *unclean* (viewing the entire person as unclean). What began as a set of laws designed to remind people of God's holiness and provision became a catalyst of exclusion and elitism.

The Jews had a phrase they would use to describe people who were unclean: *Am Ha-Eretz*. The Hebrew phrase means "people of the land" and designates a person as untouchable and unredeemable. It was commonly taught that the blind, crippled, and lame were *Am Ha-Eretz* because their deformity was the result of either their sin or the sin of their parents (John 9:1). It was understood by the religious leaders of the day that disabled people were simply getting what they deserved. The same label was also applied to the poor (poverty was considered a sign of God's displeasure) and the insignificant members of Jewish society.

If you were someone who was clean, one of the best ways to stay that way was to avoid people who were unclean.[2] The thinking of the day was that unclean people contaminate clean people, so the religious leaders of Jesus's time would stay away from *Am Ha-Eretz*. Once someone became unclean, it was hard to move beyond that label because no one who was clean would come near him or her. The Pharisees and teachers of the law had all kinds of rules to prevent themselves from being contaminated: never go into the house of a Gentile, never touch a deformed person, and never share a meal with a sinner. In Jewish society, sharing a meal with someone connoted intimacy and acceptance, so the clean would never dine with the unclean.

We have two pictures of Jewish religion in the time of Jesus. Both paint a picture of heartless religion—the good things of God turned into ways of labeling and excluding. Gentiles? They were dogs. Women? They were insignificant. The poor, the blind, and the lame? They were getting what they deserved.

Into this setting walked Jesus of Nazareth with the most radical of messages: the kingdom of God is available to everyone, right where they are, no matter who they are and what they have done. Jesus offered the revolution of God's grace, which overturned the religious thinking of the day. Jesus redefined who was clean and unclean, and what made them that way. He so infuriated the religious establishment that they plotted against him because of those whom he touched and those with whom he ate. Jesus simply broke all the rules in revealing to people the love of God.

Today, the church faces the same temptations that faced the religious leaders of the first century. As Christianity becomes increasingly mired in its traditions, we can lose the heart of Jesus in the middle of our churches and theologies. We can miss his heart for the broken and the outcast, right in the middle of all we do in his name. It is very possible (and rather easy) for us to turn into modern Pharisees—making judgments about who is clean and who is not; which sins are forgivable and which are not; and who is redeemable and who is not. In this chapter, I want to remind us of the scandalous nature of the message of Jesus.

When Love Walked the Earth

"Love" is such an abstract concept. Part of the problem stems from how we use the word. I use the same word to describe my "love" for ice cream and my "love" for my wife. If someone asks me if I enjoyed a movie, I often respond by saying, "I loved it." Is love a feeling or an act? If I do something that is loving out of duty or drudgery, is it love? For as much as we talk about the word, we are far from understanding all that it means.

For Christians, love is a person. Love is Jesus of Nazareth. If you want to know what love is, look at what Jesus did, what Jesus said, and what Jesus refused to do, and you'll know how love works and how it doesn't. Take your life and set it up next to Jesus's life: How does my life compare to the life of Jesus of Nazareth? Do I get mad at the things Jesus got mad at? Do I weep at the things Jesus wept over? If you want to know what love is, Jesus is it.[3]

That is why it is so significant that the Bible tells us that God is love. This is bigger than the idea that God is capable of love or that he loves each one of us. It means that looking at God shows us what love is like. When the Scriptures declare that Jesus is the exact representation of God's being and the fullness of deity dwells in him, then we can say love walked the earth in the form of Jesus Christ (see Heb. 1:3; Col. 2:9). If we want to know what love is and what love does, what love hates and what love values, then we look at him. He not only calls us to love but also shows us what it is like.

For the apostles, Christianity wasn't a set of doctrines. For them, the gospel was Jesus. Evangelism was introducing people to him. I wish that were what it is for us today—just bringing people to Jesus.

We see many examples of this. Love touched the untouchable, approached the unapproachable, and forgave the unforgivable. Love saw beyond the prejudice of his day into the hearts of men and women crying out for him. Love went beyond racism, sexism, and denominationalism simply to see people and what they really needed. Love wept over evil and death, celebrated life at parties and weddings, and showed us that God is much bigger and much better than we give him credit for.

Today, this revolution of love is called the church. We are the hands, feet, face, and voice of Jesus Christ to the world. To be sure, he moves outside his church, but his church is to be the primary instrument used to advance his revolution. Sadly, I think love is one of the last words anyone would use to describe the demeanor of the church today. Insecure, threatened, naïve, simplistic, mean, and shortsighted—to me, all of these descriptions would be far more accurate. We simply don't know how to carry truth and love together. We either elevate truth over love and beat people over the head with judgment, condemnation, and religion, or we are so accepting that we abandon the radical nature of Jesus's message altogether.

The "Whoever-ness" of Jesus

In John 3, Jesus has a fascinating discussion with a Pharisee named Nicodemus. In the middle of his explanation of the kingdom of God, Jesus utters what are probably the best-known words of the Bible: "For God so loved the world that he gave his one and only Son, that whoever believes in him shall not perish but have eternal life" (John 3:16).

Lost in this incredible announcement is the word *whoever*. I think this word would have had the most impact on Nicodemus. Remember, he was a Pharisee—an expert on knowing who is in and who is out, who is clean and who is not. And he hears Jesus use this amazing word: *whoever*. I can imagine what Nicodemus might have been thinking. *Is this guy serious? Whoever believes in him? Does that mean women? Gentiles? Am Ha-Eretz?* This would have been completely foreign to the religious thinking of Jesus's day.

Jesus not only preached the gospel of "whoever-ness," but also demonstrated it. He systematically approached and responded to the cast-offs of Jewish society to offer them healing, wholeness, and forgiveness. And many religious leaders hated him for it. Has much changed in two thousand years?

Many examples of the "whoever-ness" of Jesus can be found throughout Scripture. For those of us who grew up in church, the name Zacchaeus probably brings back memories of the Sunday school song about him: "Zacchaeus was a wee little man." But Luke's account of Jesus's interaction with him doesn't emphasize how short Zacchaeus was but rather how wicked he was. The song obscures what we should see in the story. Zacchaeus was a chief tax collector. He oversaw the collection of taxes on the Jewish people for the Roman government.

For the Jewish people of Jesus's day, the first portion of income or crops went to Rome. (Some estimate it was as much as 12½ percent.) Zacchaeus's job was to collect those taxes. He was also given permission by Rome to collect a percentage over that for himself (that was how the Romans bribed Jewish men into this role). He could charge as much as he wished; the Jews could do nothing about it. They couldn't complain to the local city council or vote Zacchaeus out of office.

Remember, poor people were considered *Am Ha-Eretz*. They couldn't worship or go to the temple because they were viewed as "people of the land." Zacchaeus was one of the main reasons so many Jews were poor. He was corrupt, unscrupulous, and wealthy beyond imagining. It is nearly impossible to overstate how much tax collectors were hated as a result.

Imagine that you are Jewish and that you live in Nazi-occupied Poland during WWII. You hate the Germans who occupy your country, rounding up your loved ones and sending them off to "work camps." But the only people you would hate worse than the Nazis were the fellow Jews who helped them do their work. Such was the loathing of tax collectors in the first century. They were viewed as traitors who grew wealthy at the expense of their countrymen. They not only were considered *Am Ha-Eretz* themselves, but also were viewed as the lowest scum of Jewish society (the New Testament, in Luke 15:1 for example, goes so far as to make a distinction between tax collectors and "sinners"—the former being far worse than the latter).

It is no surprise, then, that the people began to mutter against Jesus when he offered to dine with Zacchaeus; this was something rabbis simply didn't do. Jesus picked the most disgusting and vile person he could find and announced that salvation was available (and had come!) to him.

The religious system of the day taught that you had to be ceremonially clean in order to approach God. Jesus reversed this. He demonstrated that his kingdom was so "at hand" that you could approach God as you were and *he* made you clean. This was a revolution of grace! Look at those to whom Jesus ministered: the paralyzed, blind, lame, deaf, demon-possessed, Samaritans, Gentiles, Romans, women—anyone who was *Am Ha-Eretz*. Jesus was drawn to them and they to him.

In Matthew 9 we meet a woman who had a problem that caused her to bleed for twelve years. We read elsewhere that she had spent all of her money on doctors, trying to find healing. It was taught in those days that if a woman had menstrual bleeding for that long, it was the result of sexual sin and was God's judgment on her. In other words, she was getting what she deserved. Not only was she considered unclean, but she also was most likely stigmatized as well. She wasn't allowed to worship and was probably an outcast from her family. She was *Am Ha-Eretz*.

With great faith, this woman fought through the crowds to touch the hem of Jesus's robe. She didn't want to touch him directly because she thought she would infect him with her uncleanness. She didn't want him (or anybody) to notice because she was the woman with "the problem" and had been mocked and scorned for twelve years.

Yet how does Jesus deal with her? Once he realized who had touched his robe, he called her "daughter" and told her she had been healed. Instead of being infected by her uncleanness, Jesus gave her wholeness and healing. It was thought that you had to be "clean" before you could come to God. But Jesus called people to come to him and taught that then God would make them clean. The writers of the biographies of Jesus take pains to show us this. Nobody was too unclean or too sinful for Jesus. He simply received *whoever* would come to him.

If tax collectors were the most vilified members of Jewish society, then lepers were the most revolting. Matthew records an incident where a leper approached Jesus for healing. The disease itself was bad enough, but the social stigma associated with it was far worse.[4] Lepers were forced out of their homes, disowned by their families, and excluded from all forms of Jewish worship. They were not allowed to work and had to live outside their cities and villages with other lepers. They were never physically touched and were cut off from normal human contact. If they came within one hundred feet of other people, they were required to warn them of their presence by shouting, "Unclean, unclean!" Children would throw rocks at them, adults would spit at them, and the religious leaders would avoid them.

The story of Jesus's encounter with a leper is recorded for us in Matthew 8:1–4. We can almost hear the brokenness behind his request. He had been beaten down for years, a victim of heartless religion. So what did Jesus do? He touched the man! This would have been staggering to the original audience. Everybody knew that if you wanted to stay clean, you would *never* touch a leper—ever! You would steer clear. And certainly Jesus could have healed the man without touching him. But he touched him to make a point. You don't have to be clean before God will touch you; come to him, and he'll make you clean.

Can you imagine what life was like for this guy after his encounter with Jesus? Running home to his family, worshiping in the temple, and being able to feel human touch again? Can you imagine his joy?

After the leper, someone even worse stops Jesus: a Roman centurion. This would be like living in France during World War II and having a Gestapo agent drop by. Israel was an occupied country, and a centurion was like a captain; he commanded one hundred soldiers. Centurions didn't ask you for help; they would tell you what to do. You were not supposed to talk to a Gentile, let alone a Roman, let alone a soldier, let alone a leader of soldiers. Why would Jesus talk to the man? Because he saw through the prejudice of his day and saw the man's heart toward his servant who was suffering. As it turns out, this Roman had such great faith that he believed Jesus could heal his servant without even seeing or going to him. Jesus, astounded at this faith, does just that.

Casting Stones at Fellow Strugglers

We seem to believe we have to be clean—respectable or religious—before we can come to God. We believe it is possible to sin too much, wander too far, and blow it too big to come to God. Many of our churches reinforce this message. The sinners of Jesus's day were attracted to him even though his message was uncompromising. It was the religious people— the pious and the powerful—who were suspicious of him and threatened by his message.

Today little has changed. The pious and the powerful have refashioned Christianity comfortably into their own image and have lost the heart of Jesus in the process. We have said, in hundreds of different ways, that you must talk like us, look like us, and have your lives "cleaned up" like us before you are welcome. A man recently approached me with an all-too-familiar story. He believed in Jesus as a young man but had wandered away for many years. He stood at the door of our church and asked me if God was OK with his coming back! I was dumbfounded. God is more than OK with it! I pointed him to Luke 15 and the story of the prodigal son, but I grieved that he felt he even had to ask me.

How have we lost the revolution of Jesus? Since when is the church a place for people who are supposed to have it all together? When did it cease being a community for the screw-ups and the *Am Ha-Eretz* of today's society? Why do we feel that we have to have our addictions cured, our doubts answered, and our religious lives in order before we can come and fall at the feet of Jesus? When did the church become a place for those who aren't desperate and unclean?

I pray that we grasp again the revolutionary "whoever-ness" of the gospel of Jesus. He picked the most marginalized, sinful, and broken people he could find to demonstrate God's love.

Some of us need to be reminded of our own "whoever-ness." We need to be reminded that, before we met Jesus, *we* were *Am Ha-Eretz*. Many of us get so religious and church-ized after we start following Christ that we start making the same distinctions the Pharisees did: Some people are clean, and others are unclean. Some sins are forgivable, and others are not. Some people are redeemable, and others have fallen too far and sinned too much. This is Pharisaism all over again. And this is where religion, apart from Jesus, leads us. The Pharisees used religion to narrow the pool of people who were acceptable in God's sight. Many of us do the same thing. What keeps us, though, from this pride and self-righteousness is God's mercy in reminding us that we were once "whoevers," too.

Growing up, I was a good, moral kid. I didn't sneak out, didn't drink, and didn't sleep around. I got good grades, did OK in sports, and was generally liked. I grew up going to church, but I didn't see any need for Jesus because I was good. I thought, honestly, that he was lucky to have me. I was also very judgmental. Once I learned the religious system of keeping score, I (in my mind, at least) did pretty well.

But when I graduated from college, my so-called good self turned bad. I became addicted to pornography and masturbation. I got into a very physical relationship with a woman and ended up trying to end the relationship seven different times knowing it was wrong. I was lustful, money-hungry, selfish, and prideful. My "good" self was unmasked.

During this time in my life, I became a youth pastor! (Looking back on this, I can't believe my hypocrisy.) The weight of my sin finally became so great that I went before the leaders of my church to tell them how much of a fraud I was. I let them know everything. God was gracious to me—they were men of grace and truth. They called me into responsibility and accountability, and I submitted myself to their leadership and discipline. They offered me some time alone in a cabin in the woods to seek God's wisdom and forgiveness.

I had never spent that much time in solitude before, so I went with great fear and apprehension. I didn't want to face the God I had been ignoring for so long. I spent my first three days reading and memorizing the Bible, studying and journaling—anything to avoid the encounter I knew was coming.

On the third night, God did what I was afraid of. He unveiled my heart. He showed me my sin—how lust and greed and pride had taken over my life. How poorly I treated this woman I thought I loved. He showed me my heart's vileness, lostness, and darkness. He, in his great mercy, revealed to me the depths of my sin.

I broke. I sobbed. I cried out for mercy. And when it was the darkest, God's spirit cried out to my spirit that Jesus died for *me*. Not just for the sinners *out there*—but for *me*! The gospel was for me! I could be forgiven. Mind you, I had known all of this in my head before then, but the reality of it had never found its way to my heart.

And so it was there in my brokenness that God showed me my "whoever-ness." I wasn't so judgmental after that. I learned the joy of being chosen and invited and loved all at once. God needed to show me my sin so that I would not get in the way of others who wanted to come to him. I knew I could never be clean enough, but I cried out to God and he received me!

Some of us need a similar reminder. But there are others who are *too* in touch with their "whoever-ness." Many believe there is no way God could love, forgive, and redeem them. Maybe you are one of those people. Please know this: to you, Jesus is saying, "I am willing! Be clean!" He promises to save, to touch, to heal, and to forgive. We don't have to be clean first. All we have to do is come to him.

As the church of Jesus, we need to announce this from our rooftops. We dare not play the games of the Pharisees and turn the community of faith into the junior high playground. If Jesus were to walk the earth today, whom would he seek out? Who in our society would be the first to embrace his revolution? It would be the *Am Ha-Eretz* of today.

The circle of those whom God loves has always been bigger than the circle the church has drawn. That is the scandal of grace.

The Body and Blood

The body of Christ was broken and his blood was shed to forgive and cleanse all of us—even the "worst" of us. To deny this—the "whoever-ness" of the gospel—is to become modern-day Pharisees. So we proclaim this message:

For God so loved the world that he gave his one and only Son, that *whoever* believes in him shall not perish but have eternal life. (John 3:16, emphasis mine)

His body was broken and his blood shed:

For the violent
For the addicted
For the lustful
For the greedy
For the rapist
For the porn star

For the drug dealer

For the murderer

For the abortion doctor

For the unforgiving

For the jealous

For the pedophile

His body was broken and his blood was shed to redeem us all—even the worst. Do we really believe this? Do we really proclaim this? To proclaim this is to proclaim the message of Jesus; to proclaim anything else is to preach another gospel entirely.

5

THE DANGER OF THEOLOGY

When I started dating the woman who was to become my wife, I quickly began learning all sorts of information about her. We talked a lot, and I learned what kinds of food she liked, what TV shows she watched, where she went to college, and a lot about her family background. We spent hours sharing and catching each other up on our lives to that point. After ten months of dating, I became convinced that I actually *knew her*. But, as every married person will attest, there is a vast difference between knowing information about someone in a dating relationship and actually knowing *him or her* in the context of marriage.[1] All of the information I had learned about her was no substitute for what it was to be united with her in marriage and life. I got married and then realized that there was a whole lot about Justina that I didn't know. But I knew enough to know that knowing the rest would be worth it.

I think the same thing can happen in our relationship with Jesus. Because God is a personal being, it is possible to know *about* him without really knowing *him* (just like how I thought I knew my wife). This is precisely what I did growing up. I knew that Jesus lived, that he walked on water, and that he died for my sins. In college, I could give you the arguments that proved the Bible was reliable and that Jesus, in fact, rose from the dead. But I didn't know Jesus; I just knew a lot about him. I had a relationship with a bunch of facts, but I didn't have a relationship with Jesus himself.

Many of us miss the revolution of Jesus for precisely this reason. We have a relationship with a book, a set of beliefs, or a theology, rather than the living Jesus. The Jesus of Suburbia beckons us to feel content with information, not transformation; theology, not telephony. We become lulled into thinking faith in Jesus is nothing more than faith in statements about Jesus.

I see this in the church. We teach and preach Jesus but so often grow content with simply knowing *about* him instead of knowing *him*. Much of the work we do in the church is to get people to agree with information about God, Jesus, and the Bible. We call this mental exercise "belief" or "having faith." Christians often refer to other Christians as "believers," and we invite people to "believe" in Jesus (per John 3:16). But our modern, Western idea of belief is very much like my learning information about my wife. It is possible to learn a lot about Jesus but still not *believe* in him. We may even intellectually agree with the information we have been taught, but that still falls short of what the Bible means by "belief." This chapter answers the question, "What does it mean to *believe* in Jesus?"

The Limits of Theology

When Jesus walked the earth, there was a great deal of confusion about who he actually was. In Matthew 16:13–14, Jesus asked his closest followers what people were saying about him: "When Jesus came to the region of Caesarea Philippi, he asked his disciples, 'Who do people say the Son of Man is?' They replied, 'Some say John the Baptist; others say Elijah; and still others, Jeremiah or one of the prophets.' " The crowds were not quite sure who Jesus was.

In Mark 3:20–21, Jesus's family is convinced that he is crazy: "Then Jesus entered a house, and again a crowd gathered, so that he and his disciples were not even able to eat. When his family heard about this, they went to take charge of him, for they said, 'He is out of his mind.' "

The religious leaders of Jesus' day also had their doubts about him. In John 8:48, they remark about him, "Aren't we right in saying that you are a Samaritan and demon-possessed?" Samaritans were Jews who had intermarried with Gentiles (non-Jewish people) and were considered half-breed outcasts. Needless to say, neither remark was a compliment.

So here is the picture the Gospels give us. The crowds were

unclear about who Jesus was. They thought that maybe he was the second coming of Elijah or Jeremiah or that he was John the Baptist. His family at one point thought he was insane, and the religious leaders accused him of being a demon-possessed half-breed. It's clear that there was much confusion surrounding the identity of Jesus of Nazareth.

However, there was one group of beings who always recognized who Jesus was:

- Mark 1:23–24: "Just then a man in their synagogue who was possessed by an evil spirit cried out, 'What do you want with us, Jesus of Nazareth? Have you come to destroy us? I know who you are—the Holy One of God!'"

- Mark 5:6–7: "When he saw Jesus from a distance, he ran and fell on his knees in front of him. He shouted at the top of his voice, 'What do you want with me, Jesus, Son of the Most High God? Swear to God that you won't torture me!'"

It is startling to note that throughout the Gospels, demons had pretty good theology. They were the only group consistently clear on the identity of Jesus. If we define "belief" as merely mental agreement with information, then demons believed in Jesus. They not only used exalted messianic titles to describe him, but also acknowledged his power and authority over them. His family thought he was crazy, the religious leaders called him demon possessed, and the crowds couldn't agree on who Jesus was. Yet the most consistent voices proclaiming the identity of Jesus Christ were the demons that encountered him.

James makes this same point in his New Testament letter. He argues that saying you believe in something is one thing but living like you believe is often another. If your words and actions disagree, which will more loudly declare your beliefs? According to the book of James, the answer is your deeds. Actions always reveal the heart. It doesn't matter what you say you believe, because you can say anything you want. So James argues that faith, if it doesn't result in action, is not genuine faith. Such faith is dead and worthless. To help make his case, he refers to the belief of demons: "But someone will say, 'You have faith; I have deeds.' Show me your faith without deeds, and I will show you my faith by what I do. You believe that there is one God. Good! Even the demons believe that—and shudder" (James 2:18–19; the words *faith* and *belief* being understood synonymously).

Many of us understand *believing* in Jesus to mean mentally agreeing with accurate information about him. We hold that theology (the study of God) is central to faith. For most of us, "belief" means that we intellectually agree to a list of truth statements about Jesus. But if that is all there is to believing in Jesus, then we should list demons among believers in Christ. They understood who he was well before anyone else understood.

The Bible doesn't present belief this way. Having correct information about Jesus is critical, but "belief" is much deeper than that. My fear is that, as followers of Jesus, we have been lulled into thinking we know Jesus simply because we have learned a* lot of information about him. The vast majority of people in the United States say they believe in God, yet that belief makes little to no difference in how they live.² Believing Christian theology does not equal following Christ. As Mark Buchanan writes,

> To have carefully tested theology is good, but it is not the same thing as knowing God. Too often theology ends shy of love, worship and service. Too often it gets stuck in smugness, dryness and rigidity. Too often it is as impersonal as calculus. . . . Jesus' apostles were theological idiots, while demons almost always showed themselves to be astute theologians.³

I am convinced it is possible to be able to agree mentally with information about Jesus and still not know him. It is possible to be able to recite our creeds and belief statements and still not have come to accept Jesus as Forgiver and King. It is possible to have great theology and still not trust Christ. As Jesus himself says,

> Not everyone who says to me, "Lord, Lord," will enter the kingdom of heaven, but only he who does the will of my

Father who is in heaven. Many will say to me on that day, "Lord, Lord, did we not prophesy in your name, and in your name drive out demons and perform many miracles?" Then I will tell them plainly, "I never *knew* you. Away from me, you evildoers!" (Matt. 7:21–23, emphasis mine)

The Faith of Sitting

In the New Testament, *to believe* means to trust. The Greek word for belief, *pisteuo*, means to have confidence in something. Trust is basic to what it is to be human. There are not two kinds of trust: religious trust and nonreligious trust. We all trust something and someone; the only issue is whether or not the object of our trust is religious. All trust works the same way. What you believe and what you trust are always revealed in how you live and act. I know the people who sit in our church each weekend trust their chairs because they sit in them. It doesn't matter what they say; their behavior reveals their trust. I know they trust their cars because they drive them. When we look both ways before crossing the street, we are trusting in our senses to convey an accurate picture of the world. Trust always reveals itself in behavior.

Trust in Jesus is no exception; it involves much more than just mentally agreeing with information about him. Trusting Jesus, like trusting other things, should show up in how we actually live. Our typical American understanding of "belief" leaves this part out.

This doesn't mean that we never have questions or doubts. It means, simply, to be firmly persuaded in, confident of, or won over by the person of Jesus. The author of Hebrews defines faith as "being sure of what we hope for and certain of what we do not see" (Heb. 11:1). The opposite of faith isn't doubt; it is *sight*. If faith is trusting in what you can't see, then the opposite of faith is sight—only trusting in what you can see (2 Cor. 5:7).

What Belief Looks Like

To believe is to trust. It is far more radical than just agreeing with information. To know Jesus goes beyond knowing the right information about him. In the Scriptures, the people who demonstrated great faith in Jesus often had little or no information about him. They were not inundated with Christian books, TV, and radio airwaves full of Christian teaching and music, or multiple Bible translations. These people came to faith in Christ not always understanding the nuances of the doctrine of the Trinity or substitutionary theory of the atonement. According to the Scriptures, here is one example of what it means to believe in Jesus:

Now one of the Pharisees invited Jesus to have dinner with him, so he went to the Pharisee's house and reclined at the table. When a woman who had lived a sinful life in that town learned that Jesus was eating at the Pharisee's house, she brought an alabaster jar of perfume, and as she stood behind him at his feet weeping, she began to wet his feet with her tears. Then she wiped them with her hair, kissed them and poured perfume on them. When the Pharisee who had invited him saw this, he said to himself, "If this man were a prophet, he would know who is touching him and what kind of woman she is—that she is a sinner." Jesus answered him, "Simon, I have something to tell you." "Tell me, teacher," he said. "Two men owed money to a certain moneylender. One owed him five hundred denarii, and the other fifty. Neither of them had the money to pay him back, so he cancelled the debts of both. Now which of them will love him more?" Simon replied, "I suppose the one who had the bigger debt canceled." "You have judged correctly," Jesus said. Then he turned toward the woman and said, ... "Therefore, I tell you, her many sins have been forgiven—for she loved much. But he who has been forgiven little loves little." Then Jesus said to her, "Your sins are forgiven." The other guests began to say among themselves, "Who is this who even forgives sins?"

Jesus said to the woman, "Your faith has saved you; go in peace." (Luke 7:36–44, 47–50)

Jesus rarely said no to a dinner invitation. (I find that inspiring; I am always up for a free meal!) The home of a prominent Pharisee would probably have an open courtyard attached to it where the dinner party would have been held. The courtyard wouldn't be too sizable but could accommodate twenty to thirty people comfortably. A low, flat table would be at the center of the courtyard. Cushions would surround the table—the table was low enough that chairs were never used.

Meals were extravagant gatherings that would last several hours and many courses. Between each course, the guests would "recline" (lean back away from the table on their elbows) to relax and talk. So when the text says that Jesus was reclining at the table he was literally at the low table, leaning back on an elbow, and talking between courses of the meal.

A great deal of protocol went with a meal like this. Many poor people would gather around the edges of the courtyard to overhear the conversation and hope for some scraps of food. The Pharisees viewed these occasions as religious, so many rules were attached to how a meal like this would progress.

The text then introduces us to a woman "who had lived a sinful life." English doesn't do a great job of capturing how notorious such a woman would be. She had done more than just "blow it" a couple of times; she had lived a perpetually destructive life. This woman separated herself from the edge of the courtyard to approach Jesus. One of the major rules of etiquette was that "outer wall" people were not allowed to approach the center table. The fact that she was a known "sinner" made her approach especially scandalous.

Next, she started crying, and not just a little bit. She was sobbing. She ended up making a scene in front of the whole crowd. She didn't say a word but began wiping Jesus's feet with her hair. This, too, was a violation of protocol. "Proper" women in Jewish society never let their hair down in public; it was considered a sign of promiscuity. So was touching Jesus with her hair. All of this was socially out-of-bounds.

Let's recap. She left the edge of the courtyard, breaking rule number one. She completely interrupted the dinner and approached a well-known rabbi, breaking rule number two. She let her hair down (number three) and touched him, wiping his feet with her hair (number four). It is understandable, then, that Simon (the host) tried to get Jesus out of this awkward situation. In Simon's mind, it was simply inconceivable that a rabbi would allow this to happen if he really knew who this woman was. He tried to get Jesus off the hook.

Jesus's response to Simon's thoughts is staggering. He had the audacity to forgive the woman's sins, right then and there. Can you imagine the scene? Everyone around Jesus was horrified at the behavior of this "sinner," but he was delighted by her faith. We don't know if she repented or ever completed a discipleship course. We don't know if she knew all the right answers or understood the Trinity. Jesus simply announced, "Your faith has saved you; go in peace," before she even asked for it.

Jesus indicates that it was her "faith" that saved her (v. 50). Not her tears or her boldness (although both were indications of genuine faith). She didn't earn her way into forgiveness; it was given to her as an act of grace. She didn't need a lecture on how sinful she was; she knew it, and so did everybody else. What Jesus saw in her behavior was a demonstration of belief.

Was she firmly persuaded? Was she won over by Jesus? Did she trust? Absolutely. And her belief was much deeper than knowing things about Jesus—she was won over by *him*.

Please don't misunderstand me. Sound doctrine is critical to belief. So are discipleship programs and Sunday schools. But believing is bigger than these things. I wonder if we have defined believing so narrowly that there are people who think they believe, but really don't, and if there are people who've never prayed "the prayer," but still believe and will find themselves with Jesus forever. What does believing look like? Does it look like the recitation of a creed (cf. Luke 11:28)? For this woman, it looked like breaking every single social rule because she just had to get to Jesus. She was willing to risk mockery and shame and embarrassment. To the astonishment of all, Jesus responded by granting her forgiveness. Examples of this are found throughout the Gospels.

- The belief of the hated Roman centurion who immediately recognized the authority of Jesus (Luke 7:1–10) and caused Jesus to be amazed and declare, "I have not found such great faith even in Israel."

- The four friends of a paralytic who dug through a roof to lower their friend in front of Jesus (Mark 2:1–12) demonstrated great faith. In response, Jesus forgave the sins of the paralyzed man and healed him of his paralysis. We don't know anything about this guy—whether he gave money to the poor or prayed regularly. All we know is this: he was firmly persuaded and had great confidence in Jesus.

What does believing look like? Again, what does Jesus say saved them? The fact that they dug through a roof? No, Jesus pointed to the *faith* that caused them to dig through the roof. It was *faith* that caused the woman to separate herself from the wall and break every social rule. It was the *faith* of the sick woman that moved her to brave the crowds just to touch the hem of Jesus's robe (Mark 5:25–34).

The Faith of Desperation

To "believe" in Jesus, in the biblical sense of the term, we all must come to the same point. We must reach the end of our goodness and religiousness and become convinced we never will be (or can be) good enough to earn God's love. There is no possible way to be sincere enough or religious enough to please him. We have to move beyond an intellectual under-standing of our sin and his grace and into the reality of both. Biblical faith isn't for those who are content with their own religious performance. It's for those who are disgusted with who they are and what they have done. Faith in Jesus is for those at the end of their rope—those who have tried every-thing and realize nothing else can satisfy the deep needs of their soul. The kind of faith that Jesus looks for comes from hopeless, faithless, and worthless people who awaken to him.

At that point, when we really believe, it won't matter how much we'll have to dig through or how many people we'll make uncomfortable, because *there is just something about this guy, and I am willing to do anything to be close to him.*

That's belief! It's the cry of desperation and dependence. It is waking up to the beauty and majesty of Jesus to the point where we don't care if our family approves or our spouse agrees. It doesn't matter! There is something about *him*, and we'll do anything to be close to him.

The problem that we good religious people have is that many of us never get to that point. We never come to the end of our own goodness; we think God is lucky to have us. True faith, however, springs from precisely the opposite understanding. Those who encounter Jesus (both then and now) become very clear on two things: God is good, and we are not. That is what characterized those in the Gospel stories who "believed." These were the forceful people who grabbed hold of the kingdom of God (Matt. 11:12). They simply were so compelled by the person of Jesus they couldn't keep themselves from barging in.

Hitting the Jackpot

In the first century, there weren't many ways to protect your possessions. IRAs, banks, and the FDIC weren't around, so many people would simply bury their treasure in order to keep it safe. They obviously couldn't mark the location or tell others where it was located. In a region that was incredibly tumultuous, it would not be uncommon for someone to die and leave his treasure buried in the ground without anyone knowing where it was.

Jesus tells a story in Matthew 13 about treasure hidden in a field. This would not have been an unfamiliar scenario to his audience. A man came along one day and found someone's buried treasure. The text says that he went off "in his joy" and sold all he owned so that he could buy the field and have the treasure. This, Jesus suggests, is what the kingdom of heaven is like (vv. 13:44–46). And this is the attitude of the one who enters into it.

I think this is a picture of biblical belief. This is a picture of the kind of heart that Jesus responds to. Until we are convinced that there is nothing more valuable than Jesus and his kingdom, a lot of his teaching will seem like nonsense. If we come to Jesus complaining about the cost of following him, then what we really believe is that there is treasure to be found elsewhere. The people who believe and demonstrate great faith and trust in him are the people who recognize there is treasure nowhere else. This recognition, in turn, produces a joy and urgency, a hunger and desperation that cause them to be willing to do anything— dig through a roof, interrupt a dinner—just to have him.

Christians refer to themselves primarily as believers—we assent to certain things being true. We distinguish between multiple Christian denominations by pointing to differences in their beliefs. In this sense, Christians are defined by what they believe, by that to which they mentally agree. This is necessary, but it is not enough. Such "believing" merely puts us in company with demons. You can believe all the right things and still be in bondage; you can know the right answers and still be miserable and unchanged. It is possible to know much about Jesus but not really know him.

My fear is that lurking behind our American understanding of "belief" is the false Jesus of Suburbia—the Jesus who requires Christians only to agree with the truth but is not so bold as to require us to live it. Not so the real Jesus. Jesus declares in Luke 6:46–49:

> Why do you call me, "Lord, Lord," and do not do what I say? I will show you what he is like who comes to me and hears my words and puts them into practice. He is like a man building a house, who dug down deep and laid the foundation on rock. When a flood came, the torrent struck that house but could not shake it, because it was well built. But the one who hears my words and does not put them into practice is like a man who built a house on the ground without a foundation. The moment the torrent struck that house, it collapsed and its destruction was complete.

Believing can never be separated from living. The early church knew this. The followers of Jesus weren't immediately known as "Christians." Instead they were known as followers of the Way—a way of life instituted by Jesus (Acts 9:2).

Following Jesus was understood not as an act of believing but primarily as a way of living.

This reflected the teachings of Jesus. He tells a parable in Matthew 25 regarding the judgment of the world:

When the Son of Man comes in his glory, and all the angels with him, he will sit on his throne in heavenly glory. All the nations will be gathered before him, and he will separate the people one from another as a shepherd separates the sheep from the goats. . . . Then the King will say to those on his right, "Come, you who are blessed by my Father; take your inheritance, the kingdom prepared for you since the creation of the world. For I was hungry and you gave me something to eat, I was thirsty and you gave me something to drink, I was a stranger and you invited me in, I needed clothes and you clothed me, I was sick and you looked after me, I was in prison and you came to visit me." Then the righteous will answer him, "Lord, when did we see you hungry and feed you, or thirsty and give you something to drink? When did we see you a stranger and invite you in, or needing clothes and clothe you? When did we see you sick or in prison and go to visit you?" The King will reply, "I tell you the truth, whatever you did for one of the least of these brothers of mine, you did for me." Then he will say to those on his left, "Depart from me, you who are cursed, into the eternal fire prepared for the devil and his angels. For I was hungry and you gave me nothing to eat, I was thirsty and you gave me nothing to drink, I was a stranger and you did not invite me in, I needed clothes and you did not clothe me, I was sick and in prison and you did not look after me." They will also answer, "Lord, when did we see you hungry or thirsty or a stranger or needing clothes or sick or in prison, and did not help you?" He will reply, "I tell you the truth, whatever you did not do for one of the least of these, you did not do for me." Then they will go away to eternal punishment, but the righteous to eternal life. (vv. 25:31–46)

Though there is much debate about all the details of this passage, one thing is clear: Jesus is talking about how we are accountable for what we do to serve the world around us. Notice that Jesus doesn't talk about our accountability in terms of whether or not we believed well. He doesn't ask us if we had everything lined up correctly or whether we were in the correct denomination. Those are not the questions that Jesus asks. He wants to know if we fed the hungry, clothed the naked, and looked after the sick.[4]

I am not suggesting that correct beliefs are unimportant. Understanding who Jesus is and what he did for us is critical. I am concerned that we have added too many things to the lists of essentials and now require followers of Jesus to assent to a theology as part of their trust in Jesus. I don't believe this was Jesus's intent for his followers, nor was it the practice of the early church.

As I have said, the earliest Christians belonged to a movement called the Way—they were identified by how they lived, and they lived that way because they believed in Jesus. It was assumed that believing wasn't the focus; it was living according to the teachings and grace of Jesus that was the goal.

The Cosmic DMV

To close, I'd like to offer one last picture of the difference between knowing about Jesus and really knowing him. The point of this chapter has been to recognize that we must resist the temptation to tame and soften the message and demands of Jesus, thereby turning him into the Jesus of Suburbia. One of the ways we do this is by separating the mental part of belief from the trusting and active part of belief. I worry that we have called people into relationship with information rather than with the resurrected Christ himself. We have made believing the end, not living.

When I moved to California from Ohio, I was required to obtain a California driver's license. So I went down to the local DMV, picked up my study guide, and made an appointment for a couple of days later. As I began to study, I realized the test I was about to take had nothing to do with how I actually drove my car; all that was required was that I memorize the right answers so I could recognize them on the test. I didn't need to actually drive according to the test book; I just had to learn the information in it.

You'll be relieved to know that I passed with flying colors— I have always been good at memorizing information I'll never really use. In reflecting on that experience, though, I realized this is the way we present Jesus to people. Getting into heaven, we say, is like passing the cosmic DMV exam. As long as you know the right answer (which, of course, is "Jesus"), you'll pass, since it doesn't matter how you really live.

The real Jesus pictures heaven differently. He says heaven is like being invited to a party (see Matt. 22:1–14). It doesn't matter if you know the host's name (or other information about him); what matters is whether or not the host knows you.

I read this somewhere: the American church has been educated far beyond its willingness to obey. The Jesus of Suburbia would have us believe that what we need is more doctrine—if people just knew their Bibles better, we would have stronger Christians. Perhaps. I think the real Jesus would call us to something far more dangerous: to actually live the truth we say we believe.

6

ALL THINGS ARE SPIRITUAL

I am a huge fan of Christian bookstores. I have spent much time and money to feed this habit. I often drag my bored wife along with me on our dates as I browse the aisles walking right past the "How to Romance Your Wife" section. So I consider myself an expert on Christian bookstores.

I have observed an interesting trend over the years. The Christian "stuff section" (all the stuff with verses, crosses, and fishes stamped on them) is rapidly overtaking the book section. Call it trinket sprawl. It used to be that the theology section was a whole section in the bookstore. Now it warrants a couple of shelves while Precious Moments figurines take up a fourth of the store.

I've been reflecting a little bit on Christian trinkets.[1] That's what I'm going to call them. I don't mean to disparage them by calling them trinkets—there is nothing wrong with them per se, but I have been wondering why we feel compelled to stamp things with crosses, verses, and fish. If it can be stamped with a Christian symbol, someone has already done so. Christian clothing, movies, music, mints, toys, board games, superheroes, pens, artwork, jewelry, license plate covers—I even came across "Fruit of the Spirit Potpourri" (in seven different varieties, of course).

Again, there's nothing inherently wrong with this, but I wonder if it doesn't represent some bad theology on our part. Why must we stamp things as "Christian" before they are safe? Why do we have to put a verse or a cross or a fish on it before it's usable to us? What's the thinking behind that?

Similarly, why do some people believe certain jobs are "sacred" (like being a missionary or pastor) and other jobs are "secular" (like being a mortgage broker or corporate executive)? Why do we still persist in this belief even though the Scriptures clearly teach that we are all ministers in whatever ministry God has called us?

Why do we talk about our spiritual lives in purely religious terms? If somebody asks me, "Hey, how's your walk with Jesus?" I immediately want to tell them about my prayer life and quiet times, but I don't talk about my driving or how I talk to my wife when I am angry with her.

I think we very badly misunderstand the spiritual life, and because of that misunderstanding, we are confused about what it really means to follow Jesus. The false dichotomies of "sacred versus secular" and "spiritual versus nonspiritual" have been used to soften the demands Jesus places on us. He isn't merely interested in our religious lives; he wants our whole lives—everything in and about us.

It Is Good

Seven times in the book of Genesis, God declares creation to be "good." This is a powerful word that declares the joy and delight God took in making all of creation. To say that creation is good is to say that it is exactly the way God wants it: full of infinite variety, exploding with color, and delightful in all respects.

The book of Job describes a really interesting encounter between God and Job. For over thirty chapters, Job has been suffering, listening to bad advice from his friends, and asking God all sorts of questions. And God, true to form, doesn't answer any of these directly. Instead, God goes on an extended discourse pointing to the incredible beauty and complexity of creation.[2] He asks Job to consider the ostrich, the wild donkey, and the leviathan. For three chapters, God cites various aspects of creation to make the simple point that if Job can't understand what is going on in the world he can see, he won't understand what God is doing elsewhere.

One of the ideas that really comes out in God's response to Job is how absolutely delighted he is with what he has made. Have you ever seen the shows on the Discovery Channel about sea creatures that have just been discovered but have existed for thousands of years? I wonder why God created them when no one has been able to enjoy them. And then I realize that God himself has been enjoying them. That is the flavor of the book of Job: we realize what creation means to God. He delights in what he has made even if it serves no discernible purpose. The Scriptures reveal a God who regards every single aspect of his creation with great joy.

Spiritual Dirt

In Genesis 2, the account shifts away from the creation of all things to the creation of man and woman. Verse 7 says, "The LORD God formed the man from the dust of the ground and breathed into his nostrils the breath of life, and the man became a living being." The Hebrew word for "breathed" is a lot like the Hebrew word for "spirit." These words are related. This verse is suggesting that God made man a spiritual being by breathing life into him. Human beings are more than lumps of dirt—we are fundamentally spiritual beings.

Human beings are unique in all of creation because we are both physical *and* spiritual beings. Animals and plants are physical beings that are not spiritual in nature. On the other hand, angels and demons are spiritual beings that are not physical. They could have bodies, but bodies aren't essential to their nature.

Human beings are different creatures altogether. In a human person, the physical world and the spiritual world are forever joined. That's why the Bible's teaching on the resurrection of Jesus is so important (beyond validating Jesus's ministry): we will live forever in bodies. Human beings are the kinds of beings who have bodies. The Scriptures declare that we don't live without bodies in heaven; we receive new ones (1 Cor. 15:35–49). Having a body is a good thing. God created the world and called it good. He created human beings to be spiritual beings in physical bodies.

This background is necessary to understand that, over the course of church history, one of these aspects of being human has been emphasized over the others. At times the role of the body in spiritual life has been highlighted to the neglect of the growth and formation of our souls and hearts, while at other times the pendulum has swung in the other direction, downplaying the fact that we are physical creatures. The current Christian culture of the West has stressed the ideas of "spiritual discipline" and "spiritual formation." While this has been a needed correction to years of emphasizing outward behavior in obedience to Christ, there is one major trade-off I wish to discuss. The point of this chapter is simple: all issues are spiritual issues. All disciplines are spiritual disciplines. We can't separate the spiritual from the physical, and much of our teaching on the spiritual life of following Jesus attempts to do just that.

Real Life Is Spiritual Life

What the Hebrew people understood, and what we must re-learn, is that because we are both physical *and* spiritual beings, there is no issue that isn't in some way a spiritual issue. How you use your body is a spiritual issue. How you dress your body is a spiritual issue. How you speak to people is a spiritual issue. How you react when you are angry, how you use your money, how you play and work and marry—all of these are spiritual issues. The Jews understood the entire world as spiritually relating to God because we are funda-mentally spiritual creatures.

This is critical to understand because so much of our teach-ing on what it means to follow Jesus depends on getting people to do "spiritual" disciplines: Bible reading, solitude, fasting, service, prayer—these are all necessary and vitally important disciplines. But they are not the only ways we express spiritu-ality, nor are they the only disciplines that are spiritual in nature. Because I am a spiritual being, the way that I drive is an expression of loving my neighbor, and the way I talk with my wife when I am angry is a better indication of my spiritual condition than whether or not I had a devotional time that day.

As I was learning about how to follow Jesus, I never heard it this way. I thought following Jesus was a matter of being "religious" and learning to do "spiritual things" like pray and go to church. This understanding of the spiritual life, however, didn't include most of what I did during the day: working, studying, dating, playing, driving. I was taught that some things were spiritual, and other things weren't; some things were sacred, and other things were secular. So I assumed Jesus was interested only in the "spiritual" or religious parts of my life. I didn't know he wanted the whole thing.[3]

I have another problem with the idea of spiritual disciplines. The phrase itself seems to imply that there are some disciplines that are not spiritual—and that is dangerously false. I don't dispute that Bible study and prayer and church are important things. They are essential. But when they are emphasized as being the only (or the most important) spiritual activities in which we engage, then Christianity leaves the rest of our lives untouched.

The Jews would have looked at what we Christians call a "time with God" in the morning and called us crazy. They viewed their whole day and everything in it as "time with God." God doesn't just listen to the little bit that you pray to him, he listens to your whole life. You don't have your time with God and then go on to something else.

Most of us read Paul's encouragement to "pray continually" (1 Thess. 5:17) and say, "Oh, I'll never be able to do that." The Hebrews, however, did exactly that. They had a blessing to pray over every little bit of life. They prayed a blessing to God thanking him for the ability to go to the bathroom without pain. Seriously. You prayed blessings on birthdays, feasting days, and fasting days. Blessings for sunshine, blessings for rain, blessings for great food, blessings for bad food, blessings for poverty, and blessings for wealth. They fundamentally under-stood that *your whole life mattered to God*—not just this little part that we want to call the religious part of us.

The All-Encompassing Way of God

When God revealed his heart for the nation of Israel and how they were to live as his chosen people, he didn't just give them the Ten Commandments. He gave them hundreds and hundreds of regulations, rules, and rituals that encompassed all of their lives. Take a look, for example, at the laws in the book of Leviticus.

- In Leviticus 11—Laws concerning clean and unclean food
- In Leviticus 12—Laws concerning purification after childbirth
- In Leviticus 13—Laws concerning infectious skin diseases and mildew
- In Leviticus 14—Laws concerning cleansing from skin diseases and mildew
- In Leviticus 15—Laws concerning bodily discharges

You get the point. God deals with sexuality in chapter 18; money, interest, and wealth in chapter 25; and in chapter 19, we find various laws concerning haircuts, tattoos, business, clothing, neighbors, parents, and how to treat disabled people. The way of God for the people of Israel was all encompassing—nothing was left out. If you were to follow God, you were to *align your entire life with God*. Every issue was considered spiritual.

In Genesis 1, God said being created is good. In Genesis 2, God makes human beings spiritual creatures, nestles them in this environment, and gives them laws that govern their whole lives. This is so important because many of us live with the false understanding that some things are sacred and other things are secular—that only some things are spiritual. God's word declares exactly the opposite. Rather than asking, "Hey, what does this thing have to do with God?" the Hebrews would ask, "What doesn't have to do with God in one way or another?"

Jesus never called us to be believers—he calls us to be followers who believe. It was so easy for me to be a Christian early on because I thought the whole thing was an exercise in *believing*. But following Jesus is an exercise in *living*—because we believe. When we think most of our days are spent doing things that are not spiritual or sacred in God's sight, we subjugate Jesus to simply being our forgiver. But he is more than that. He is Lord, King, and Teacher. He is interested not just in redeeming my sins, but also in redeeming my *real, whole life*.

Jesus Christ is interested in you and your whole life—your

problems, friends, family, job, and weaknesses. He's interested in your real personality. It's you he wants to save, and it's your whole life he wants to redeem. He wants it all surrendered to him—your work, your play, your relationships, your speech, your body, your dress, the way you buy things, what you do with your money—he wants it all.

When I look at my day, how much of my twenty-four hours is spent worshiping, praying, reading, or sharing my faith? What about laundry? Playing in the pool with my son? Changing my daughter's diapers? What about all that I do that doesn't seem religious or spiritual? Much of the current teaching on spiritual growth seems to suggest that these are less spiritual pursuits than the religious ones cited above. But Scripture says no such thing. In fact, Scripture teaches and assumes that all issues are spiritual issues and all disciplines are spiritual disciplines. This is the key to spiritual growth: the recognition that all aspects of my everyday life can be done for the glory of God and used by him to shape me more and more into the image of Jesus.

New Gnosticism

Before we explore this further, I want to turn our attention to one of the most dangerous teachings confronting the early church. Called Gnosticism, this teaching held (I oversimplify a bit) that the universe was divided into two realms: the spiritual and the material. The spiritual world is vastly superior to the material world. Matter—the physical stuff we are made of—is inherently evil. In other words, being created was not "good." Gnostics taught that God, who is pure spirit, could not have (and would not have) inhabited a material body because matter itself is contaminated. Moreover, Gnostics suggested that there was something fundamentally wrong with being human—having human desires for food, drink, and sex. To be sure, these desires have been tainted by the fall, but nowhere does Scripture suggest that all of the goodness of God's creation has been "pushed out" by the effects of sin.[4]

The Gnostics denied the truths of Genesis 1 and 2 and argued that the material part of being human was bad while the spiritual part of being human was good. They understood human beings to be spirits "trapped" in physical bodies and couched the salvation that Jesus offers in terms of releasing humans from their bodies.

Although Gnosticism was thoroughly refuted by the early church, its effects still lingered. Of particular interest was an idea that developed during the Monastic period of church history: to really serve God, one must withdraw from the realities of everyday life and be cloistered in a monastery focusing on the things that are spiritual. To have possessions was OK, but if you really wanted to serve God, you would embrace poverty. Marriage was tolerable, but if you really wanted to devote yourself to the spiritual life, you should take a vow of chastity. Even though the doctrine changed, the effect was still the same: there were spiritual activities and unspiritual activities, and most of the time, real life was deemed unspiritual.

Several New Testament writers counter this view. Paul deals with this false teaching in a couple of places. In 1 Timothy he writes:

> The Spirit clearly says that in later times some will abandon the faith and follow deceiving spirits and things taught by demons. Such teachings come through hypocritical liars, whose consciences have been seared as with a hot iron. They forbid people to marry and order them to abstain from certain foods, which God created to be received with thanksgiving by those who believe and who know the truth. For everything God created *is good*, and nothing is to be rejected if it is received with thanksgiving, because it is consecrated by the word of God and prayer. (4:1–5, emphasis mine)

What Paul is saying here is significant. He is arguing that the entrance of sin and death into the world didn't push all the goodness out of it. Creation is still good. Paul also says that followers of Jesus must receive things with thanksgiving and consecrate them with the word of God and prayer. This, of course, doesn't mean that everything is good if we pray over it. There is no way to purify porn and make it into a good thing. When Paul says that we are to consecrate things through the word of God and prayer, he is saying that the stuff that passes through these filters is usable for us to enjoy. It doesn't have to be stamped with a verse, a cross, or a fish. By declaring creation to still be good, Paul was countering the Gnostic teaching that urged people to abstain from good things in the name of being "spiritual."

Paul deals with this again in Colossians 2:20: "Since you died with Christ to the basic principles of this world, why, as though you still belonged to it, do you submit to its rules?" And he starts quoting some of the rules of these false teachers: do not handle, do not taste, do not touch. Paul says these rules are "all destined to perish with use, because they are based on human commands and teachings" (v. 22). This is all Gnostic stuff, and Paul deals with it head on. Look at verse 17 of chapter 3: "And whatever you do, whether in word or in deed, do it all in the name of the Lord Jesus, giving thanks to God the Father through him." Or consider 1 Corinthians 10:31, where he says, "So whether you eat or drink or whatever you do, do it all for the glory of God."

We must see the significance of what Paul is saying. If eating and drinking are spiritual issues, then so is everything else. If words and deeds are to be used to glorify Jesus, then so is everything else. Against the Gnostics, Paul argues one simple truth: all issues are spiritual issues; everything can be done to the glory of Christ.

Back to Trinkets

Remember trinkets? In the beginning of the chapter, we asked the question, "Why do we feel we have to stamp things with crosses and fish and verses to make them safe?" I think the answer is that we have a Gnostic hangover—we haven't been able to get over the idea that some things are spiritual and others aren't. So we stamp things with crosses and label things "Christian" in order to make them safe for us to use and enjoy. We declare some work to be "secular" and other work to be "sacred," and we talk about our spiritual lives as if God were interested only in the religious parts of our lives. Behind all of this thinking stands the false teaching of Gnosticism.

We don't need fish and verses and crosses to make things sacred and safe for us to enjoy. Genesis records that "God saw all that he had made, and it was very good" (1:31). As a follower of Jesus, I am already free to use and enjoy art, music, work, and recreation, even if it is not expressly labeled "Christian." Conversely, not everything tagged with the label of "Christian" is good, right, or holy. The fact that "the whole earth is full of his glory" (Isa. 6:3) suggests that I can see and worship Jesus in just about anything.

I have had people ask me how I started into "full-time ministry." My response is that I became a Christian. All followers of Jesus are in full-time ministry—as moms, mortgage brokers, students, and clerks (see Eph. 4:12–13). I happen to get paid by a church, but that doesn't make my job any more sacred than another. The idea that there are "secular jobs" is nowhere in the Bible. It is a Gnostic leftover. What did Paul say? "Whatever you do, whether in word or in deed, do it all in the name of the Lord Jesus, giving thanks to God the Father through him" (Col. 3:17). There aren't jobs that are sacred and jobs that are secular. There are simply jobs, all of which we are to do as unto the Lord.

All of life is spiritual, and Jesus demands that it all be surrendered to him. This means that mowing your yard, carpooling, how you treat your kids, how you discipline them, how you spend your money, the whole thing is to be submitted to Christ and done for his glory.

Walking with Jesus (otherwise known as discipleship) becomes not a matter of learning to do a bunch of new religious things; rather, it means doing the things I have always done but doing them differently. I still eat, drink, work, play, drive, shop, and love, but I do those things from a new perspective. I thank God for all his gifts; knowing the Giver makes the gifts all the better. I learn to do things with excellence "in the name of the Lord Jesus," knowing he is with me at all times and is pleased when I offer my ordinary life to him for his glory. I begin to pay attention, for the whole earth is bathed in God's glory, and I recognize there is nowhere I will be that he hasn't been first. Following Jesus becomes learning to recognize and worship him in the small avenues and adventures of real life.

That is the mystery of growing to be like Jesus: he is interested in reorienting our entire lives to him, not just the parts of our lives we call "spiritual" or "religious."

A quote from Lawrence Kushner summarizes this chapter nicely:

Classic Hebrew has no word for spirituality. (The modern Hebrew, *ruchaniyut*, comes from our English word.) The English word spiritual means immaterial and connotes the religious. The concept comes to us with the heavy baggage of early Christianity that divides the universe into material and spiritual. This tradition teaches how to leave this gross material world and get to the other real, spiritual, and, therefore, holy one.

Judaism sees only one world, which is material and spiritual at the same time. For Judaism all things—including, and especially such apparently non-spiritual and grossly material things as garbage, sweat, dirt, and bushes—are not impediments to but dimensions of spirituality. To paraphrase the Psalmist, "The whole world is full of God" (Ps. 24:1). The business of religion is to keep that awesome truth ever before us.

Spirituality is that dimension of living in which we are aware of God's presence. "It is being concerned with," in the words of Martin Stresler, "how what we do affects God and how what God does affects us." It is an ever-present possibility for each individual. Jewish spirituality is about the immediacy of God's presence everywhere. It is about patience and paying attention, about seeing, feeling, and hearing things that only a moment ago were inaccessible.[5]

7

MYSTERY AND PARADOX

As a teacher of the Bible, I have often succumbed to the temptation to think that my job every weekend is to take the vastness and mystery of God in Scripture and break it into nice, thirty-five-minute, bite-sized, understandable chunks. Most of the time, it seems like a pretty noble undertaking. There has developed around the teaching profession a whole industry designed to help us in the process. We have books of illustrations, ready-for-pulpit Internet sermons, and books and DVDs on a whole range of issues. We have Bible answer men and women, apologetic Web sites to answer our toughest questions, and sermon manuals that plan an entire year of teachings for us.

On the whole, I have been grateful for all the help. But something significant has been missing.

Mystery. Paradox. Wonder. Awe. Call it what you want, but it is missing from most of our teaching and congregations. As Marva Dawn puts it:

The most critical issue facing Christians is not abortion, pornography, the disintegration of the family, moral absolutes, MTV, drugs, racism, sexuality, or school prayer. The critical issue today is dullness. We have lost our astonishment. The Good News is no longer life changing. It is life enhancing. Jesus doesn't change people into wild-eyed radicals anymore; He changes them into nice people.[1]

One of the core assumptions of the whole teaching endeavor is that it is the teacher's job to remove mystery. If you want to know God's will, here are three easy steps. Want a healthy marriage? Here are five proven principles. Need to know why God allows suffering? Here are a couple of pat answers.

This whole sermon industry has developed to do our thinking for us. And in the process, we have taken much of the inscrutable, gigantic, and mysterious word of God and attempted to make it all palatable to the masses.

Most congregations expect this. People come to the church for answers, not more questions. But, ironically enough, raising questions was central to the teaching ministry of Jesus. In the Gospels, Jesus was quite happy to raise more questions than he answered, and often, on the whole, he didn't directly answer the questions posed to him.

Instead of removing mystery, God seems to introduce and reinforce it. Instead of alleviating tension, Jesus liked to increase it.

Spiritual Growth at IKEA™

Nowhere is the temptation to remove mystery greater than in the area of spiritual growth. If we grant that all issues are spiritual issues and if we recognize that the goal of walking with Jesus is being transformed to be more like him (cf. Rom. 12:1–2; 2 Cor. 3:18), then we are still left with many questions. How do we grow in our faith? What does spiritual growth look like? What is our part, and what is God's part in the process?

We are witnessing the rebirth of an emphasis on spiritual formation in the American evangelical church. Whole shelves of bookstores are devoted to the study of how we grow spiritually. The term *spiritual disciplines* is no longer foreign to our Christian vocabularies.

And yet the church looks pretty much the same as the world around it. For all of our talk of transformation, we see very little evidence of it.

We are usually told that Jesus helps us to grow through a process. And, much like the easy three-step approach we mentioned earlier, spiritual growth usually involves several steps. Join a small group. Read the Bible every day. Pray a lot. Give your money to the church. Share your faith. Go to church and serve there. Don't cuss or get drunk or sleep around. Don't be addicted to porn or shopping.

These are all good things. Reading the Bible and praying are huge things. So is avoiding the sin that so easily trips us up. This, however, is usually all we are told. Just do these things and avoid these other things, and you will grow to be like Jesus. Maybe.

I want to suggest that one of the ways we substitute the Jesus of Suburbia for the Jesus of Nazareth is in the way we look at spiritual growth. We talk about it as if it were up to us and as simple as following a set of one-size-fits-all instructions. There is no mystery in any of this; in fact, it seems like just the opposite.

There is no doubt that God uses spiritual disciplines like these to help us grow. They are incredibly important. The problem with this whole conversation, however, is that it takes all the mystery out of what spiritual growth is and how it works.

We, on the other hand, talk about spiritual growth like we are putting together furniture from IKEA. Here is step one, then step two, then step three—the instructions should work for anybody, and if they don't, you are not following them correctly.

The Bible never talks about spiritual growth this way. As we saw in the last chapter, the Bible declares that all issues are spiritual issues and that all disciplines are spiritual disciplines. But knowing that doesn't cause us automatically to grow to become more like Jesus. It does help us, however, to see that growing to be like Jesus plays out in places that aren't just the "religious" places in our lives. It is much bigger than that.

I hope to move us from a putting-together-furniture view of spiritual growth into the idea that God often uses mystery, paradox, tension, and even his own "hidden-ness" to grow and stretch us beyond ourselves into Christ. Mystery, reverence, and paradox are what is needed in our churches, not more information or steps. An appreciation of the majesty, vastness, goodness, and providence of our holy God would serve us better than yet another book on the Rapture. We need more God and less doctrine. The problem is that God never presents himself to us as clearly as our theologies would have us believe. The great and mighty God of the Bible never fits neatly into our language, experience, history, or belief systems. This is why we must hold these things so loosely and never declare them finished.

The Formless God

Moses meets this unfathomable God in Exodus 3 in the form of a burning bush. As the story unfolds, Moses discovers he has been chosen to be God's instrument in delivering the nation of Israel from Egypt and slavery to Pharaoh. Moses has many objections, and the text indicates that God patiently answered each one. Moses's strangest request comes in verse 13, "Suppose I go to the Israelites and say to them, 'The God of your fathers has sent me to you,' and they ask me, 'What is his name?' Then what shall I tell them?"

This request makes little sense to us since God had revealed himself to the Israelites prior to this. But we must remember the religious climate of the day. Egyptian religion worshiped many gods—the god of the harvest, the god of fertility, the sun god, the moon god, the god of death, and so on. If you wanted your child to be born safely, you would appeal to the god of fertility. All of these little gods had names, and you could call upon them and make sacrifices to them depending on what you needed.

Moses had been raised in the house of Pharaoh and had received an Egyptian education. He would have known all the names of the Egyptian pretender gods, how they worked, and what they were used for. With this in mind, it was natural for Moses to assume the God of Israel would operate the same way. His name would tell Moses how God worked. Except that God doesn't play by the same rules. He answers Moses:

> "I am who I am. This is what you are to say to the Israelites: 'I AM has sent me to you.'" God also said to Moses, "Say to the Israelites, 'The LORD, the God of your fathers—the God of Abraham, the God of Isaac and the God of Jacob—has sent me to you.' This is my name forever, the name by which I am to be remembered from generation to generation." (Exod. 3:14–15)

The descriptive *I am who I am* can also be translated, *I will be what I will be*. Both the extended phrase and the shortened *I am* are derived from the Hebrew verb *to be*. In other words, God answers Moses's questions by calling himself *I exist*, as if to say, "In contrast to other pretend gods, I actually am. I really exist." This was completely antithetical when compared to the religious system of the day. By naming himself, God declared them false.

Then God gave Moses the name that he and the Israelites are to use in reference to him forever, LORD. This word is the English approximation that comes from four Hebrew consonants YHWH (or some translate it YHVH). LORD shares the same root as I AM but is in the third person. So God refers to himself as I AM and asks the Israelites to call him YHWH, which means "He is."

It is fascinating to note that God doesn't defend himself or tell Moses any more than that. He simply announces that he is. YHWH is a name of great power and mystery. It is used over 6,800 times in the Scriptures and is a constant reminder of how huge, mysterious, and awesome God is. God should do nothing but grow bigger in our understanding.

When YHWH freed his people and led them to Mount Sinai, he had Moses stand at the top of the mountain to receive the Law. The mountain was shrouded in smoke and fire, lightning and thunder enveloped the region, and the people were so frightened that they asked God to stop speaking to them and to speak only to Moses (Exod. 20:18–19; Heb. 12:18–21).

When, in Deuteronomy, Moses reminds the children of Israel about that event, he tells them several times that God revealed himself without form:

Then the LORD spoke to you out of the fire. You heard the sound of words but saw no form; there was only a voice. . . . You saw no form of any kind the day the LORD spoke to you at Horeb out of the fire. Therefore watch yourselves very carefully, so that you do not become corrupt and make for yourselves an idol, an image of any shape. (Deut. 4:12, 15–16)

The significance of God appearing without form lies in the second commandment prohibiting the Israelites from making an image of the unimaginable and formless God. In other words, when God revealed himself to the whole nation, he never did so in an image that could be turned into an idol and worshiped. God knows our hearts; had he revealed himself in a specific way, through a certain image, we (like the Israelites) would have been tempted to worship the image, rather than the reality.[2]

In spite of Moses's warnings, the people became fearful when Moses spent forty days away from them with God on the mountain. They decided to make an image (of a calf, which had great religious significance in their region) and worship that as YHWH. The text says that after the calf was formed, Aaron announced to the Israelites that there would "be a festival to the LORD" the next day (Exod. 32:5). I had always assumed that the golden calf represented a *different* god, one more to their liking. But many scholars believe that the calf was their representation of YHWH. They were not comfortable with how big and terrifying he was without Moses around, so they constructed an image of him that was more comfortable and less demanding.

Throughout the Scriptures, God gives us constant reminders of his vastness and majesty. He reveals and invites us into relationship, but he never allows us to forget how big he is. In the Old Testament, his name served that purpose. So did the fact that he appeared to people without form. But the Israelites couldn't handle a God that awesome, and they set about, time and again, to reduce him to a more manageable size.

This has *always* been the temptation of the people of God—to tame him. He increases mystery; we desire to remove it. He introduces paradox; we seek to solve it. We, like the Israelites before us, want a God who is understandable and predictable and safe. We want a God who makes sense and operates according to generally accepted accounting principles. But instead, we meet YHWH and his son, Ye'shua, who don't play by our rules.[3]

Our problem in nice and tidy consumer America is that we want God to do things we understand and when he does and we are pleased with what he is doing, then we'll worship him. But God declares that he is YHWH and we are to worship him whether we understand him or not. We have made a god out of our intellects. We worship God only when he makes sense. God reveals himself as a God we will never figure out. And yet we can know him intimately. That paradox is what sets us free.

It is in the times of questioning, doubting, wondering, and

worrying that our faith is tested and grows. We are not huge fans of true mystery and paradox. We like mysteries that resolve themselves neatly at the end. We don't like tension; we like resolution. We like the comfortable clarity of the Jesus of Suburbia over the ravenous wonder and fear the real Jesus brings.

One of the things God uses to make our faith more mature is the fact that we can't figure him out. He is so much bigger than we make him out to be. We see this most clearly in the biblical account of a man named Job. Job's faith progressed through three stages, from immaturity to maturity, and God used mystery and paradox and tension to bring him from one stage to the next.

Faith in Faith

Job was an incredibly righteous man of God. The Bible says he was "blameless and upright." He was also very wealthy. The book of Job begins by giving us a glimpse into his faith:

His sons used to take turns holding feasts in their homes, and they would invite their three sisters to eat and drink with them. When a period of feasting had run its course, Job would send and have them purified. Early in the morning he would sacrifice a burnt offering for each of them, thinking, "Perhaps my children have sinned and cursed God in their hearts." (1:4–5) This was Job's regular custom.

Job was so concerned with pleasing God that he even offered sacrifices for his children, just in case they had sinned. We see throughout the book that the predominant paradigm for understanding God was this: If you do good things, God will reward and protect you. If you do bad things, you will suffer and be punished (see Job 34:11). It was that simple. It is no coincidence that the book of Job opens by telling us that Job was both godly and rich—that was how it was thought to work.

This is something that I call having faith in faith (which is much different from having faith in God; we'll get to that in a moment). Job was very religious, and his religiousness was based on what he was receiving from God. His faith wasn't in God yet; it was in *his* own ability to please God through *his* religious activity. His faith rested in his religious performance. That was why he sacrificed to God on behalf of his children.

As the book continues, we overhear a conversation in heaven held between God and Satan about Job:

> "Does Job fear God for nothing?" Satan replied. "Have you
> not put a hedge around him and his household and everything
> he has? . . . But stretch out your hand and strike everything he
> has, and he will surely curse you to your face." (Job 1:9–11)

Satan immediately recognized the arrangement: Job was good, so God blessed him. Satan's question amounted to this: What would happen if God quit blessing him? Would he still be good? In other words, was Job faithful to God because of what he received from God, or was Job faithful simply because he trusted God? This question is at the heart of Job's faith.

Having this kind of faith isn't necessarily a bad thing. It's just not the mature faith God wants from his children. It is a furniture-building faith. This faith amounts to a contractual arrangement between God and me: I do good works, and God blesses me.

There is no joy or peace in this kind of faith because whether or not we receive God's blessing ultimately rests on us. We have to get everything just right; we have to offer sacrifices for our children just in case they blow it. Many of us have this kind of faith.

God gives Satan permission to wreak havoc on Job's life (which raises all sorts of interesting questions), and Job loses everything. Reflecting on this, Job says, "What I feared has come upon me; what I dreaded has happened to me" (Job 3:25). What was he referring to? What was it that he feared? I believe it was the fear that God would someday remove his blessing from Job's life.

Job was afraid because he was ultimately trusting in a system. That is what is so appealing (and dangerous) about this stage of faith. It is simple and clear. If I do X, then God will do Y. I reduce my relationship with him to a contract, an agreement, or an equation. There is no mystery here. And that is the way most of us like it. When I first started following Jesus, I needed formulas, simple principles, and easy steps. I needed clarity to deep questions. People who have faith in faith want to escape from mystery, not run headlong into it.

For the rest of the book, Job's friends encourage him to trust the system. You are suffering, they say, so you must have done something wrong. They remind Job of the system and that all he has to do is quit doing evil and God will bless him again.

Dismantling the System

In the midst of all his suffering, Job never gave up on God. In Job 13:15, he declares, "Though he [God] slay me, yet will I hope in him" (see also Job 6:10; 19:25). Even his wife advised him to abandon his faith. Through it all, Job stayed faithful to God. But he did give up on the system. He no longer had faith in faith. All that he thought he knew was kicked out from underneath him. Throughout the book, Job defends his righteousness and pronounces himself innocent of any wrongdoing (e.g., Job 13:13–21), and God does vindicate Job in the end (Job 42:7–9). So why did he suffer? That is the question Job poses. If God blesses the righteous, and he was righteous, then why did he suffer when he had done nothing wrong?

It is in this questioning of God that we see the maturation of Job's faith. God purposely introduces paradox, mystery, tension, and suffering into Job's life in order to dismantle the religious system Job had set up. Everything Job had hoped to gain through his religious performance (what we are calling "faith in faith") was lost.

God sometimes, it seems, lets our systems crash, not because we've done something wrong but because he has something better for us.

Job hung on to his faith, even in the midst of the most trying of circumstances. He never accused God falsely. He complained and groaned and wrestled with God, but he never gave up. Not everybody does this. When we reach this point—when we can no longer trust in our systems of faith to protect us from harm and mystery—many of us turn away from God. We don't want to trust him, we say, because it didn't do us any good. Many people are out there blaming God for not being the religious vending machine they'd hoped for.

It is in this desperate place, where our understandings of God have been overturned and when our world has been knocked upside down, that we realize the truth: many of us are religious precisely to keep us from trusting God. We go to church, we give money, and we do all the right things—in the hope that God will never put us in a position where we actually have to trust him.

God often uses mystery and paradox and pain to help us grow. At times God hides from us or thwarts our best efforts to build a life without him (see Isa. 45:15). It is precisely when we don't have it figured out, when all of our "right answers" become nothing more than sand castles against the waves of doubt and wonder, that God does some of his best work.

This is the place where we have to trust—not in answers

but in *him*! How much of our religion is designed to keep us from such a place? How much of our Christianity is designed to keep God at arm's length—to con him into giving us what we really want? How much of it is used precisely to keep us from this point? I would rather trust a book or a system or my religious performance than trust God.

Why do I give my money to the church? Do I really do it as an act of reverent obedience in recognition that all that I have is God's? Or do I give so I can trust in the fact that I have paid God off—he owes it to me to take care of me? When it comes to money, do I trust him, or do I trust the fact that I give to him? The idea is that my religion, my faith, can be used to try to shrink God down to size and to keep me from really trusting him. We want our spiritual growth to be under our control, and one of the things God does is remind us that he can't be figured out.

Faith in God

So God allows our nice, neat systems and theologies to crumble. Sickness invades our bodies. Our finances go south. Our loved ones walk away from what is good and right. All of this forces us to move into trusting God. Often God has to bring us to the point of desperation so we will learn how to trust. This is where Job ends up.

His religious system has been destroyed and his theology reduced to dust. God allowed Job to enter into incredible desperation. And it was all because God had something better in mind for him.

The move from having faith in faith to faith in God is a painful one, but well worth the journey. Faith in God is the kind of faith that says, "It doesn't matter if God answers my questions or removes my pain. I am content with him." At the end of the book, God makes an appearance: he comes to Job in the form of a whirlwind. This is what Job had been after the whole time—to see his God.

God does not answer Job's questions. As we have already detailed, God declares his glory and mystery by pointing Job to the features of the physical world. As God says, though Job can see them, he cannot understand them, so he should not expect to understand the unseen things God is doing in the world. As God says through the prophet Isaiah, "As the heavens are higher than the earth, so are my ways higher than your ways and my thoughts than your thoughts" (Isa. 55:9). With this, Job is satisfied. All of his religiousness and questions fade into nothing. He has encountered his God, and that is all that mattered. Job responds to God in chapter 42:

I know that you can do all things; no plan of yours can be thwarted. You asked, "Who is this that obscures my counsel without knowledge?" Surely I spoke of things I did not understand, things too wonderful for me to know. You said, "Listen now, and I will speak; I will question you, and you shall answer me." My ears had heard of you but now my eyes have seen you. Therefore I despise myself and repent in dust and ashes. (vv. 1–6)

We see several things in Job's response. We see that Job understood that there is mystery to God and that all of his previous understanding about how God worked had been wiped away. Job recognized his insignificance in the face of the awesomeness of God. He repented by ceasing to use his religious system to manipulate God into making everything right. For Job, faith in God came when God met Job in Job's desperation. Once his nice religious understanding had been demolished through his suffering and circumstance, all Job had left was faith in God. There was nothing else to hold on to.

We can now see clearly the difference between faith in faith and faith in God. Faith in faith seeks to avoid mystery and pain. Faith in God comes when we see God in the midst of mystery and pain, when God strips us of our props and religious manipulations and reveals himself to us in the midst of our emptiness. When Job announces, "My ears had heard of you but now my eyes have seen you" (Job 42:5), he affirms his faith in God regardless of what he gets out of it. His vision of God was so great that he saw it really didn't matter what had happened to him. When that happened, the element of desperation went out of his faith. And having seen God, he saw that whatever needed to be taken care of would be taken care of.

There must come a point where each of us chooses to follow God, not for our benefit but because we were made for him. We must each cease striving and bargaining with God to remove all pain and mystery from our lives.

We don't like mystery because mystery forces us to trust and wait and be patient. Mystery is painful. Mystery and patience are certainly not the American way. We have one-minute Bibles and fifteen-minute inspiration messages and little trinkets with Bible quotes on them. We want to grow, we want to do it now, and usually while doing something else at the same time.

Living the Journey

For years now I have tried to please God, driven not by a desire to always bring him glory through my life, but often by the system of faith in faith. I gave money to the church so that God would always provide; I waited to have sex so that I could have a great sex life when I was married; I pray for my kids every day to guarantee they will turn out well. I confess to having pursued God for his benefits, but not for him. There are benefits to following God, of course, but they became my sole focus. If I were just good enough or religious enough or sincere enough, God would protect me from mystery and pain.

I had my nice, tidy theologies, and I practiced my simple, clear religious system. I worshiped the Jesus of Suburbia—the Jesus who made sense, who wants nothing more than to make me happy. It wasn't until the bottom dropped out of my life that my faith grew to the point where I actually trusted God. Up until then, all my religion was just a convenient way of avoiding the trust that came from desperation.

God, in his infinite mercy and firm tenderness, demolished the neat system I had set up. He broke his part of the arrangement. I have experienced nothing so bad as Job (or as many of you), but my world crumbled from the inside out. Mental illness became a phrase I used to describe how I was doing. Depression and fear became core elements of my internal vocabulary. I have always been a hard-charging, smooth-talking, Type-A driven kind of guy, and I was knocked flat by the breakdown of the lies and schemes that had been forged out of pain long ago.

And then I saw God. Not the way Job did. (I only wish it were that dramatic.) But I saw him most clearly when I had nothing else to fall back on—not religion, not theology, not performance or friends or family—just him.

Here's what I learned. Our boxes, our language, our finite minds are simply not big enough to comprehend the true and living God. We are most in danger when we think we have him figured out. How does God grow people? Often by reminding them how big he is and how small we are. By introducing mystery and tension and difficulty into life so that we might be forced to move beyond trusting our faith and religious systems to actually trusting him.

I encourage you to take a bold risk: ask him to do this in your life. You'll see him, and you'll never be the same.

8

THE CHURCH AS
SUBVERSIVE COMMUNITY

What comes to mind when you think of the church? For some, the word brings painful memories; far too many have weathered a church split or denominational breakup, or have been mistreated, forgotten, or disillusioned. For others, church conjures up memories of Easter or Christmas, or maybe a wedding or two. For them, church is a building where religious people do religious things. For me, when I was younger, it was a requirement: church was what I had to endure on Sunday mornings when I would rather have been sleeping in. I had to get dressed up, sit in an uncomfortable pew, sing songs to weird music, and listen to a speaker talk about things that had no connection to my everyday life.

Not surprisingly, God had none of this in mind when Jesus ordained the church to carry on his work in the world. Much of the scorn toward Christianity from those outside our faith comes from the seeming hypocrisy of the Christian community. This is a far cry from Jesus's statement that the world will know we are his disciples by our love for one another. The church was to *be* an object lesson, revealing Christ to a lost and unbelieving world. Yet the church today often obscures him. What would it look like to be the church in a way that actually reveals Jesus to people?

The Church and the Mall

Consumerism is the god of this age. I spend my days choosing between countless goods and services, all designed to cater to my preferences and whims. I wake up in the morning and have my choice among an absurd number of breakfast cereals (or other breakfast foods, for that matter). I can catch up on the news either by reading my choice of newspapers, by checking any number of Web sites, or by watching one (or more) of two hundred TV channels. I stand in front of my closet looking at over thirty different shirts (although I usually just wear my top four), thirteen pairs of shoes, pants, shorts—most of which I don't need, let alone ever wear. I drive to work listening to one of one hundred radio stations. I go out to lunch at my pick of hundreds of local restaurants, each offering an extensive menu of selections. Going to the mall or grocery store presents me with a bewildering array of choices. I spend all day, every day, deciding what I want and what will be most pleasing to me. When I choose poorly, I have "buyer's remorse"; when I choose well, I feel momentary satisfaction until I have to look into my overstuffed refrigerator and decide what to have for dinner. My life is based on my right to choose.

So it is no surprise that this mentality creeps into the church. Many of us come to God with our wants, desires, and preferences in primary view. And churches, if they are not careful, begin to cater to the perceived demands of their patrons. A mall mentality infects the church. We feel the need to offer a dizzying selection of services and ministries designed to "meet the needs" of the whole family, realizing, of course, that if we don't, there are many churches in the area who are willing to meet those needs. Our job, even unconsciously, becomes outdoing the "competition" down the street.

Erwin McManus, in his book *Unstoppable Force*, makes a distinction regarding the church, which has stuck with me. McManus distinguishes between the church as a *movement* and the church as an *institution*. A movement is concerned with its mission—it exists for a reason and will stretch itself to grow and accommodate to fulfill that mission. An institution, on the other hand, exists for itself—it seeks to maintain the status quo and usually has a great deal of resistance to change. A movement adapts and grows; an institution preserves and guards. A movement is organic and grass roots; an institution is structured and hierarchical. This distinction exists on a continuum—every church, to some degree, is both movement and institution.

God intended his church to be a movement, guided and

powered by the Holy Spirit to fulfill the mission of Christ on the earth, which is to make disciples of all nations and to be his witnesses to the ends of the earth (Matt. 28:18–20; Acts 1:8). Both structure and organization are necessary within such a movement. We see this in the early church and the instructions of Paul. The apostles had to delegate some work to others so they could focus primarily on teaching and prayer (Acts 6:1–7). Paul put believers in positions of authority and charged them with oversight and leadership of local churches (e.g., Titus 1:5).

Not everything about an institution is bad, but I suspect most of it is simply unhelpful in accomplishing the mission the church has been given. When the church turns inward and begins catering to the preferences of those who are there, it leaves the dynamic edge of Spirit-led obedience to places of greater and greater discomfort. When a church spends most of its time on cherished traditions and ceases to ask God in prayerful dependence what else he may be doing (even if it doesn't look like what we are doing now) so that we may join him there, we lose the joy and wonder of seeing God do the unexpected and unplanned-for.

Many of us realize the consumer mindset is the exact opposite of the outlook we are to have when it comes to the purpose of the church. I've heard many times, "The church is the only organization that exists for its non-members." Most agree with the sentiment; we just don't know how to do that or why. The church has been (and still should be) a revolutionary community attempting to subvert and redeem the culture around it. Perhaps the clearest picture of how the church should function within a culture that is hostile to it comes from the book of Revelation.

The Unveiling of Jesus

The book of Revelation is either the most obsessed-over book in the Bible or the most ignored. With its evocative imagery and thundering declarations of the majesty and supremacy of the one true God, the book of Revelation has been fodder for Christian imaginations for thousands of years. The current popularity of the *Left Behind* series of books is proof enough of that.

The theology behind most of the current teaching on Revelation is dangerously adrift from its Old Testament roots and original first-century context. The book is primarily a letter to seven real, flesh-and-blood churches who existed in the first century in what was then the Roman province of Asia. One of the most fundamental mistakes many commentators make in understanding the book of Revelation is forgetting that the book would have made sense to its original audience. Its symbols, imagery, and hundreds of Old Testament illusions would have been readily understood by Revelation's first-century hearers (see Rev. 1:3).[1]

The seven churches of Revelation existed during the time Rome ruled the known world. From England to India, Roman power and culture held sway. Jesus Christ and the movement that bears his name were born into the mightiest empire the world had ever known. From its origins, the revolution of Jesus was subversive of the propaganda that poured out of Rome (as I discussed in chapter one).

Emperors called "Caesars" ruled the Roman Empire. They gradually began to see themselves as divine—literally gods on earth. Some of them demanded to be called "lord and god" and "king of kings and lord of lords" and required their subjects to bow in worship before them.[2] Against the Caesars of Rome, the earliest Christians proclaimed that *Jesus* was Lord and ruler of the universe. They proclaimed that the name of *Jesus*, not the name of Caesar, was the only name under heaven by which men and women could be saved.

The early Christian churches were called Ekklesia—a name borrowed from assemblies that had for years been formed to worship Caesar. These Christian Ekklesia were countercultural and subversive in nature. Whereas the world at that time divided the world into male and female, Jew and Greek, slave and free, the movement of Jesus announced, "There is neither Jew nor Greek, slave nor free, male nor female, for you are all one in Christ Jesus" (Gal. 3:28). While Caesar would announce himself as the provider for the poor and the giver of bread, the early church would gather, often in secret, to worship God by taking care of its poorest members and celebrating the bread and cup of Jesus (see Acts 2:42–47; 4:32–35). This is why Luke makes sure to remind us that "there were no needy persons among them" (Acts 4:34). The early church subversively cared for its own and the least of Roman society.

The newborn church of Jesus stood against the deification of Rome at an increasingly great cost. By the time Revelation was written, Christians were beginning to lose their lives for their refusal to bow down to Caesar (see Rev. 2:13). Rome grew progressively more hostile to the movement of Jesus, and Revelation was written to the church to encourage, to inspire, and to call for perseverance in the midst of the hostile culture around them.

Revelation is a book about Jesus Christ. In fact, the first sentence of the book in English begins this way: "The revelation of Jesus Christ . . . ." *Revelation* means "unveiling"—the revelation of Jesus Christ is the unveiling of Jesus Christ. The whole book declares, through pictures and symbols, the absolute majesty and divinity of Jesus Christ over all things. The book is not primarily a blueprint to the "end times"; rather, it is the most exalted presentation of Jesus in the Bible.

As this exalted Jesus walked among his churches, he reprimanded some of them, encouraged others, and demonstrated a great passion for the faithfulness of his church. One church needed to restore its first love; others were facing persecution and death. Some were dealing with false doctrine and idolatry; others were wrestling with sexual sin and church discipline. Some were spiritually rich but physically poor, while others were physically rich but spiritually poor. Jesus called all of those churches, regardless of what was going on within them, to *overcome* (see Rev. 2:7, 11, 17, 26; 3:5, 12, 21). To overcome means to conquer, redeem, and be victorious in the struggle against culture. This call of Jesus must have seemed incredible to the small house churches spread throughout Asia Minor as they considered the might and majesty of the Roman Empire. But in little over three hundred years, this tiny movement of Jewish peasants would find its way to the very center of the religious system of Rome, for better and worse.

We discover what it means to overcome when we see the picture of Jesus presented to us in Revelation 5. We are told in verse 5 that "the Lion of the tribe of Judah, the Root of David, has triumphed [overcome]." These exalted titles come from Genesis 49 and Isaiah 11 and evoke a strongly militaristic and nationalistic image of the Messiah of David. This is the Messiah the Jews expected, a mighty warrior king who would conquer nations and destroy the enemies of God's people. This is what John *heard*: he heard about the conquering Messiah. Now, verse 6 says he *looked*: "Then I saw a Lamb, looking as if it had been slain." He heard about a lion and looked and saw a lamb. He *hears* about a lion that has overcome but *sees* a lamb that was slain. What he saw was the lamb whose sacrificial death had redeemed people from all nations (Rev. 5:6, 9–10). The Lion was also the Lamb.

Revelation 5 presents us with a new symbol of conquest and overcoming: sacrificial death. Jesus conquered not by force but by death, not by violence but by martyrdom. He came not to be served but to serve and give his life as a ransom for many.

The image of a lamb would have been very familiar to the Jews of the day. From Exodus 12, when God called Israel to an annual sacrifice for Passover, lambs were the picture of powerlessness and sacrifice. Jesus is presented in the New Testament as our Passover Lamb (see John 1:29; 1 Cor. 5:7; 1 Pet. 1:19).

I want to examine this paradox. Jesus calls his churches to overcome—to engage and redeem and be victorious over the culture around them—and then shows them what this looks like. This is one of the paradoxes of our faith—that Jesus conquered and overcame through suffering and sacrificial love. The lion conquered by presenting himself as a lamb. While he was being crucified, he was establishing his invisible and indestructible kingdom.

As we consider what it means to be the church in the midst of a hostile culture, this is the picture Jesus used time and again. A savior willing to suffer. A God willing to serve. A Messiah who would seek and save the lost. A lion who is also a lamb. To engage, subvert, and redeem culture is to live in this paradox. It is to announce and demonstrate the message of Jesus with such radical and unconditional love that we become lambs in the process. The picture of Revelation is not only for the churches of the first century, but also for the church today. We are called to overcome and then are given a picture of the One who has overcome, and this reveals what the church's posture should be to the world.

Jesus Christ founded a movement, not an institution; a community, not an organization. Movements exist for reasons outside themselves; institutions exist to perpetuate themselves. There is absolutely no question, whether in the Gospels or the book of Acts, that Jesus intended his people to work and live for something beyond themselves. The early believers understood that they were the hands, feet, voice, and face of Jesus to the world around them. They were at his disposal.

Who Is Our Enemy?

As tempting as it must have been for the early church to view Rome as its enemy, Revelation takes great pains to remind it of the darkness and evil that stood behind Rome and that was far greater in power. We meet the real enemy in Revelation 12, the ancient serpent called Satan, who appears as a great red dragon waiting to devour the coming Christ. In order to wage war on the followers of Jesus, the dragon gives power to a "dragon stood on the shore of the sea" and a "beast coming out of the earth" (Rev. 13:1, 11). Both beasts are oblique references to the Roman Empire and the Caesars who govern it, but the text is clear that the dragon stands behind it all, warring against Jesus and his followers (Rev. 12:17; 13:1–18). This is consistent with Paul's statement that our battle is "not against flesh and blood" (Eph. 6:12).

Rome was not the real enemy, nor were the Caesars. Satan himself stood behind them both. As much as we are tempted to view culture or individuals as our enemies today, this text reminds us of the greater conflict being waged around us and our place in that conflict. Our bosses, annoying neighbors, immoral movie stars, and cultural icons—none of these are our real enemy. They may be used by the enemy, but they are not the enemy. Our enemy isn't the ACLU, Democrats (or Republicans), the feminists (or pro-lifers), the liberal media elite (or Fox News); our enemy is the one who stands behind everything that wars against all that is good. Satan is the one who still lies and tempts and accuses.

We wage war against the dragon, but we prefer more obvious targets. Why? Because we can see the carnage when we hit them. It is easier to think my enemy is my ex-spouse or my kids or Madonna. They, at least, I can see.

This is one of the reasons the church is so ineffective in engaging and redeeming culture: we think people are the enemy. So we fight people and try to hurt them in the process. It's the pornographers or the abortionists or the courts that are at fault. We think the problem is *out there*—in the culture—when in reality the enemy lurks right in *our* midst.

We complain about not being allowed to have the Ten Commandments in our courtrooms, yet how many of us have them posted in our churches (or how many of us do what they say)? We lament the absence of prayer in schools, yet how many of our churches are truly prayerful? We think it is the *culture* that is growing more secular, but I think it's the church! Because we have wrongly identified the enemy, he is within our gates, pulling us toward compromise and irrelevance, focusing our attention on secondary matters while the dragon himself wages war against our marriages, our kids, and our sexuality.

As an example, while much attention has been given to homosexual marriage, this issue isn't the one that is the greatest threat to the institution of marriage. The real threat is the fact that the divorce rate in the church is equivalent to that in the culture at large. If there were visible differences between those who call themselves followers of Jesus and those who don't, we might not spend as much time picketing and legislating. It would be obvious to all that we have something better, something found nowhere else.

I am not suggesting that we shouldn't be politically active and aware or battle for the sanctity of marriage and the right to pray in our schools. I think these are important issues and must be fought for. But our attention to those things should never outweigh the reality of the spiritual world around us and our adversary's attempts to thwart the church from being the salt and light Christ intended.

How Do We Overcome?

Not only must we fight against our true enemy, but we are also called to overcome him the same way that Christ did (see Rev. 12:10–11). The image of martyrs around the throne of God in Revelation is consistent: it is the image of those who understand that they wage war in the same manner as Christ—through sacrificial love and perseverance through suffering. Jesus's victory makes ours possible. We are then called to reenact it as we engage and seek to redeem the culture around us. We become lions who are lambs. We become agents of grace and truth. We simply love those around us to death. We tell them the truth; we refute false ideas, but we love people as Jesus did. Our overcoming is no different than his.

To me, this isn't great news. I love that Jesus carried his cross, but I would rather not carry my own. The way of the cross is love, sacrifice, and suffering. The way of the church is often arrogance, superiority, and judgment. It is easier simply to condemn the world around us than try to redeem it.

We are to stand against the evil and falsehoods of the world with Christ as our model. He died for those he loved, and we're expected to do no less. That is revolution. That is what the church is to be. When the culture declares that the gospel of Donald Trump is the real path to happiness, we announce (and show with our lives) that joy is found in generosity and simplicity. When the world advocates power and control, we advocate (and live) service and sacrifice. It is not revenge, but forgiveness. It is not divorce, but reconciliation. It is not status, but humility. In all these ways, we stand against the world and its false gods, but we do so in great love.

Frederick Nietzsche once commented, "He who fights with monsters might take care lest he thereby become a monster." In other words, be careful, or we may become the very thing we are fighting against. We need to be reminded often of this warning. When we stand outside of homosexual unions and shout, "God hates fags!" we have become the dragon. When we murder abortion doctors in the name of God, we have become the dragon. When we insult, belittle, and slander the people who oppose us, we become the dragon. The demonstration of the gospel—the living it out in real life—isn't optional. And it is what the world is begging for: truth backed up by love, lions who are lambs.

Why is it that the Christian community insists on making so many harsh and condemning statements about the world and its people? A whole cottage talk radio and TV industry has formed around Christians relentlessly attacking and judging sinners around us, further convincing ourselves that the problem with the world is "out there" and that we, the church, are free from blame. This is not the task, or even the right, of the church. Didn't Paul say, "What business is it of mine to judge those outside the church? Are you not to judge those inside? God will judge those outside" (1 Cor. 5:12–13). It is vital to remember that the sternest words of warning and correction found in the Bible are always directed toward the people of God, not toward the unbelieving masses.

The purpose of the church is to live the purposes of Christ: to seek and save the lost and to give its life as a ransom for many. This has radical implications for the mission and function of the church. How many of our churches are revolutionary communities standing in love against the Caesars of the world? How many of our churches exist solely to advance the kingdom in the hearts of those who haven't yet been brought into it? Why do so many of our churches feel like support groups of the victims of heartless culture and like bastions of judgment and condemnation of the world instead of gatherings of insurrectionists being equipped to wage war on the world with love and truth?

We subvert culture and redeem it when we serve it in love and sacrifice. This is diametrically opposed to the consumer mindset we discussed at the beginning of this chapter. What would the world think of us if we stopped demanding our way and started laying down our lives and living sacrificially?

Dying to Live

The refashioned Jesus of the American church—the Jesus of Suburbia—would have us live a life of leisure and comfort, escaping the trouble and distress around us. But the real Jesus, the Jesus before whom John falls face down at the beginning of Revelation, would have no such thing. The hope of Christ isn't the removal of suffering and the manifold miseries of this fallen world but rather the hope that with Christ we can endure anything that befalls us. This is the testimony of the book of Revelation: thousands upon thousands of people would rather die than deny their God. Martyrs, we call them. The word *martyr* means "witness." People who have been witness to the love and power of Jesus are not willing to give him up.

For so many, the words of Jesus on this matter are ignored or explained away. It is simply impossible to follow Jesus and continue to live a life based on self-interest:

The man who loves his life will lose it, while the man who hates his life in this world will keep it. (John 12:25)

Anyone who does not take up his cross and follow me is not worthy of me. Whoever finds his life will lose it, and whoever loses his life for my sake will find it. (Matt. 10:38–39)

For whoever wants to save his life will lose it, but whoever loses his life for me and for the gospel will save it. (Mark 8:35)

Whoever tries to keep his life will lose it, and whoever loses his life will preserve it. (Luke 17:33)

Many of us may never literally have to put our lives on the line for Jesus Christ. We are still called to be martyrs. A central theme of the book of Revelation is that unbelievers were won over for the kingdom by the sacrificial death of the witnesses and by God's validation of them. Evil is conquered not by force but through sacrificial love from lions who are lambs.[3]

Martyrdom sounds so far away, but we are confronted with opportunities to die for our faith every day. In my marriage, what I watch on TV, how I treat people—all of these are opportunities for martyrdom. Every time you are obedient to Jesus in faith, you war against the dragon and demonstrate the power and love of God. Loving your enemies, blessing people who insult you—this is not a passive, wishy-washy kind of love; it is violent resistance to the powers that govern this world. We overcome and redeem by the power of the cross, the love of God, and the willingness to die even for our enemies. This is not pacifism; it is the most aggressive battle on earth— between a kingdom that is earthly and one that is not.

The kingdom of God conquered when Paul and Silas sat singing and praising God in a Philippian jail cell. The kingdom of God conquered when Peter and John refused to stop telling people about Jesus after they had been flogged. The kingdom of God conquers when house churches in communist China sing at the top of their lungs, heedlessly disregarding the threat of prison. The kingdom of God conquers when college students in Orange County, California, spend their Thursday nights ministering to prostitutes in Los Angeles. It conquers when a couple who could settle for divorce fights for reconciliation. It conquers when families open their homes to foster kids, turning their own families upside down so other children may know the love of God. It conquers when churches do fundraisers for the poor and not just bigger and nicer buildings.

You cannot follow Jesus of Nazareth without first learning how to die. This is true for us and true for our churches.

One of the things that must die is the idea that God exists to give me what I want. I must die to the notion that my life is still my own. My preferences, my dreams, and my ambitions, must all be put to death if I truly follow Jesus. In order to present ourselves as "living sacrifices" as Paul urges us, we must each come to the end of ourselves (Rom. 12:1).

Imagine if our churches were filled with such people. What would happen if we no longer spent our time catering to the already convinced and instead leveraged the best of our resources toward loving the world with sacrificial grace and truth? The answer is simple. We ourselves would overcome and bring countless others with us.

THE REDEMPTION OF CULTURE

Regardless of how you see it, we are witnessing a massive cultural shift. Call it postmodern, antimodern, or whatever. It is clearly post-Christian. The Christian community is now dealing with a new and different set of questions and assumptions from the culture around us. As the culture around us continues to change, one of the most pressing issues Christ followers are facing is how to respond. What does it look like to engage a postmodern, post-Christian culture? How should we relate to the world around us as it grows increasingly hostile to our point of view?

Assumptions

I am assuming, of course, that such a thing as "culture" really exists. Whether this concept is defined as "high" culture or "pop" culture or understood in terms of shared values, ideas, or experiences, my understanding and experience is that none of us lives in a vacuum. Each of us is immersed in and surrounded by the unseen forces of the culture. To what degree culture shapes us is debatable; that we are enculturated is beyond dispute.

Broadly defined, a "culture" is the set of ideas, values, and concepts that are jointly held to be true, right, and good by a group of people. Such cultural norms are often neither explicitly stated nor defended; they are simply assumed. The cultural shift away from modern Christian culture to post-modern, post-Christian culture is well under way and has significant implications for the articulation and defense of the Christian gospel.

The fact that culture shapes us is good and bad. It is good because it reminds us of the power of being salt and light and of using what God has done for us to bless and influence others. It reminds us that the role of the church is to invite the world around us into celebration of what is good and right and true. We can use culture to affect the world around us. We work in entertainment, political, legal, and academic fields because we know that to change culture is to change how people really live. (We also recognize that changing culture is also a matter of changing people.)

The bad news is that culture is often energized by the dark powers and principalities of which Paul speaks. In other words, the wicked aspects of culture are greater than the sum of individual sin. There is a systematic and structural evil that pervades our world. When Scripture forbids followers of

Jesus to be friends with the world or to love the things of this world, it is this part of culture—the dark and wicked part— to which this refers. Nowhere does Jesus ask us to separate ourselves completely from the world around us (John 17:15). Instead, we are to form countercultural communities in the midst of despair and evil and to engage the culture around us.

Fortunately, the question of how to engage culture is not new. The early church faced hostile persecution and resistance to its message. Jesus modeled for them, and for us, how to engage a culture that is increasingly antagonistic.

One of the burning questions of Jesus's day concerned the Roman occupation of Israel. What were the Jews to do? Had God not promised that one day they would be free? When would their deliverer come? How should they resist Roman attempts to force Greco-Roman culture and religion upon them?

The Jews were divided on the answers to these questions. Some, like the Essenes, withdrew into isolated and ascetic communities in the desert. They were convinced that the Roman occupation of Israel was Israel's due punishment for not keeping the Law, so they devoted themselves to it with absolute purity, hoping their faithfulness would encourage the coming of the Messiah.

The Pharisees shared this hope. As the popular party of the middle class, the Pharisees separated themselves from culture differently than the Essenes did. The word *Pharisee* means "separated one" and refers to the distinctive teaching of this sect of first-century Judaism. They believed that though they could not withdraw completely from the culture around them, they could separate themselves from its polluting elements. As we have seen, in most cases this led the Pharisees to separate themselves from the unclean and sinful people around them.

At the other end of the spectrum were the Sadducees, the most blatant collaborationists with the government of Rome. They were Hellenized Jews who followed humanistic philosophy (e.g., they did not believe in miracles or an afterlife). Their power and wealth grew as they aligned themselves with Rome; as a result, they had the most to lose from a change in the status quo.

The Zealots, on the other hand, were not content to wait for God's intervention. They advocated armed revolt against their Roman occupiers. Zealots led numerous failed revolts, all in the hope of delivering Israel from her foreign oppressors.

Within these groups, we can see three general ways of relating to culture: embracing it (Sadducees), withdrawing from it (Essenes and Pharisees), or simply attempting to take it over (Zealots).

As we listen to discussions today about how Christians should relate to culture, we can pick out similar positions. Some, like the Amish and the Mennonite communities, attempt to withdraw from culture completely. To a lesser degree, many evangelicals seek to withdraw from culture by forming a Christian subculture with its own schools, music, novels, movies, et cetera.

Still others in the Christian community seem seduced by modern values and ideas, and have therefore abandoned the ancient moors of the Christian faith to excise those parts of the Bible that are offensive to modern ears. They are the collaborationists of this age.

Against the modern-day Essenes and Sadducees, today's Zealots no longer advocate armed revolt but rather use political and legal power to attempt to return the West to its "Christian" roots.

Many of us fall in the middle; we are bewildered as to how we should respond. Most of us settle for being good, church-going, religious people, trying to do the best we can.

Interestingly, Jesus had little to say on the subject. Even though this debate was intense and passionate in his day, Jesus's only direct response to the many questions of his contemporaries was, "Give to Caesar what is Caesar's and to God what is God's" (Mark 12:17). But how he lived and interacted with culture is a wholly different story. He did not withdraw from culture (like the Essenes), nor did he seek to embrace it (like the Sadducees). He did not advocate armed revolution (as did the Zealots). He simply sought to *redeem* culture wherever he found it.

Jesus modeled for us that people and culture could be redeemed. Redemption involves making something acceptable in spite of its negative qualities or aspects. In other words, redemption occurs when something that previously had no value is made valuable. The story of redemption, of course, is all throughout the Bible. God redeemed and used murderers (Paul, David), drunks (Noah), prostitutes (Rahab), liars (Abraham), cheats (Jacob), cowards (Peter), the self-righteous (Jonah), and the sexually unfaithful (David, Solomon). There is no question that God can and does redeem people. But we also see from the examples of Jesus and Paul that he wants to engage and redeem culture as well.

In this chapter and the next, I will discuss what it might look like for the followers of Jesus to engage and seek to redeem the culture around them. There are no easy answers or formulas but rather ways of orienting our hearts and minds to the culture around us, while remaining faithful to the message and methods of Jesus.

Relevance and Observation

In order to engage and seek to redeem the culture around us, we must first attune ourselves to its messages and assumptions. This is precisely the posture Paul assumes in the book of Acts:

> Paul then stood up in the meeting of the Areopagus and said: "Men of Athens! I see that in every way you are very religious. For as I walked around and looked carefully at your objects of worship, I even found an altar with this inscription: TO AN UNKNOWN GOD. Now what you worship as something unknown I am going to proclaim to you. The God who made the world and everything in it is

the Lord of heaven and earth and does not live in temples built by hands. And he is not served by human hands, as if he needed anything, because he himself gives all men life and breath and everything else. From one man he made every nation of men, that they should inhabit the whole earth; and he determined the times set for them and the exact places where they should live. God did this so that men would seek him and perhaps reach out for him and find him, though he is not far from each one of us. 'For in him we live and move and have our being' [from the Cretan poet Epimenides]. As some of your own poets have said, 'We are his offspring' [from the Cilician poet Aratus and also Cleanthes]." (Acts 17:22–28)

This speech is a brilliant study in observation and relevance. Paul clearly adapts his message to his audience. In contrast to his speech in chapter 14, where he is speaking to Jews, Paul never quotes the Hebrew Bible. He begins from a point of common ground and then builds to the message of Jesus. Paul is clearly familiar with the Stoic and Epicurean philosophy of the day, and much of his speech is a point-by-point refutation of their views, while pointing to Jesus Christ as the fulfillment of them.

The lesson for our purposes is that *context matters*. This is why we must assume the posture of intentional observation. The Scriptures give us great freedom in adapting the eternal and unchanging truth of Jesus to fit into the culture and custom of the day. In other words, the good news about Jesus can (and must) be contextualized into culture.

We see this most clearly when we examine the similarities and differences between the biographies of Jesus: Matthew, Mark, Luke, and John.[1] The first three contain much of the same material, with varying emphases, while the fourth seems entirely different. Both the similarities and differences of the Gospel accounts can be almost entirely accounted for in terms of the context of their original audiences. Luke writes to Greeks and takes time to explain Jewish customs and words, while Matthew writes to Jews and refers extensively to Old Testament prophecy and its fulfillment. Both proclaim Jesus as God and Messiah, but both do so with context in mind.

From the evangelistic speeches in Acts to the biographies of Jesus, the message of the hope of Christ has always been contextualized into culture in order for it to be communicated effectively. Thus, it is possible to change the cultural "dressing" of the gospel while retaining its eternal truth.

We should bear in mind that we are capable of the reverse: contextualizing the message of Jesus so much that it ceases to be *his* message. But this should not deter us from finding innovative and relevant ways to communicate the truth of Jesus to new generations and cultures, all the while remaining faithful to what has been handed down to us.

Observing and listening to culture allow us to properly contextualize the message of Jesus so that it is heard effectively (see Eph. 5:15–16; Col. 4:5–6). I have learned this lesson firsthand.

I can point to many personal examples of the consequences of not adopting this posture. Instead I would like to share one time where, by God's grace, I think I got it right. I love going into college dorms, offering free pizza, and doing a simple presentation of the claims of Jesus, followed by a free-flowing segment of question and answer. Instead of pretending to be Bible answer man, I invite the students to explore the doubts and concerns they have about Christianity and the church. I have done close to one hundred of these, and I love them! Invariably, I end up learning more than anyone else.

One of these forums particularly stands out in my memory. It was in a women's dorm, and over sixty women showed up that night, the vast majority of whom held a non-Christian perspective. After presenting the message of Jesus, the issues of abortion and feminism immediately came up. How, they asked, could they trust the Bible when it had been used to subjugate women for centuries?

One approach certainly could have been to open the Bible to Psalm 139, Jeremiah 1, and other passages that the Christian community uses to argue against abortion. But as I listened to their arguments and concerns, I realized that there was such deep-seated distrust of the Bible that any use of it as an authority was going to fall on deaf ears.

Instead, I took a different tack. I argued that abortion on demand was not the victory for women's rights that it claimed to be but instead was a capitulation to patriarchy. Why is it, I wondered, that the Playboy Foundation is one of the biggest supporters of abortion on demand? Is it because of their deep and abiding concern for the equality and objective value of women, or is something else behind it? I argued that our current system legitimates male irresponsibility by allowing men to merely offer to pay for the "procedure" if their girlfriend gets pregnant; if she chooses to keep the child instead, he is off the hook.

Further, I argued, today's practice of abortion on demand allows schools and corporations to remain unfriendly toward moms through restrictive maternity leave and childcare policies. How can we proclaim abortion as the victory of feminism when it forces women to have surgery in order to be equal to men? (For more on this, visit http://www.feminists-forlife.org.)

I then went through the biography of Jesus and argued that he was truly the world's first feminist (if by *feminist* we mean one who argues for the equality of the sexes, not their sameness). On multiple occasions, Jesus radically subverted the first century's understanding of women and elevated them to their rightful place alongside men. I concluded by saying that the only legitimate basis for equality was not found through evolution's emphasis on survival of the fittest but rather through the declaration of Genesis 1:27: "So God created man [humanity] in his own image, in the image of God he created him; male and female he created them."

I'll stop here because I am in danger of making myself look more intelligent than I really am. Suffice it to say that after the issue had been addressed this way, we had a productive, four-hour conversation about the Bible and the church and Jesus Christ. Had I gone a different way in response to their questions, I don't think our dialogue would have been nearly as productive.

All Truth Is God's Truth

From behind our fortress of objective, absolute truth, Christianity has traditionally been defended with a "we're right, you're wrong," "us versus them" mindset that alienates, divides, and threatens. Such a paradigm is unbiblical and wrongheaded. Might there be truth in other religions? Is the gospel threatened by acknowledging that truth—that beauty and goodness exist outside of the Christian community?

Jesus clearly met people where they were and engaged them at their level. He was constantly in trouble for hanging out with the wrong people in the wrong places (How else does someone get the reputation for being a drunk and a glutton?) and engaging them with the uncompromising truth of his message.

Paul, likewise, engaged people where they were. In the passage we looked at earlier (Acts 17), he quoted Greek philosophy and poetry to argue for the truth of Jesus Christ. Don't miss this. He quoted people whom *the Greeks* considered authoritative to prove his point. He did this consistently in his speeches. If he was speaking to Jews, he quoted the Old Testament; if he was speaking to Greeks, he quoted their philosophers. Paul engaged them on their terms. He used truth wherever he found it to argue for the gospel of Jesus.

One reason my spiel on abortion was effective was because I was quoting well-known feminists who make these arguments. My audience considered feminists the credible authorities on the issue, not the authors of the Bible. Paul and Jesus do the same thing: they keep their audience in mind. In disputes with the Sadducees, Jesus quoted only from the Torah (the only part of the Hebrew Scriptures they considered authoritative). Paul affirmed statements from Cretan prophets, Greek drama, and, as mentioned above, Greek poetry and philosophy (Titus 1:2; 1 Cor. 15:33).

Residing in our inspired Bibles are the words of people who did not know God or Jesus and yet said things that were true. The moral: engaging the culture around us means that we claim truth wherever we find it.[2]

Paul made this case to the Corinthians in his first letter to them. Several different leaders and teachers ministered to the church. Some preferred Paul, as he was the founder of the church at Corinth. Others preferred Peter (Cephas) because he had actually seen the Lord Jesus and walked with him around Palestine. Still others favored Apollos, who was a dynamic teacher who came in to encourage the church when Paul left. Paul rebuked the Corinthian Church for the divisions that were forming around the preferred teachers of the different groups within the church. And then he made the following point: "So then, no more boasting about men! All things are yours, whether Paul or Apollos or Cephas or the world or life or death or the present or the future—all are yours, and you are of Christ, and Christ is of God" (1 Cor. 3:21–23). What he is saying is that all truth is ours, regardless of who speaks it. Whether from Paul, Peter, or Apollos, it makes no difference. As has been said, all truth is God's truth.

Do we believe there is truth outside the formal doctrines of Christianity? I think the answer must be yes, there is. There is truth in math, geography, science, and philosophy— disciplines that are not labeled "Christian" disciplines. Does the Bible teach us about atoms and quarks? It does not. Can we learn truth outside of the Bible? Absolutely! Paul stated this flat out in his speech to the people of Lystra: God "has not left himself without testimony: He has shown kindness by giving you rain from heaven and crops in their seasons; he provides you with plenty of food and fills your hearts with joy" (Acts 14:17). The heavens themselves show the glory of God (Ps. 19:1), and we can know him from what has been made (Rom. 1:20). John calls Jesus the Logos, the ordering principle of the universe. How big does that make Jesus? Paul tells us that in Jesus everything hangs together (Col. 1:17). Isn't it correct, then, to say that Jesus is everywhere?

With this in mind, we may argue that anytime someone comes into contact with truth, goodness, and beauty, they are coming into contact with Jesus Christ. They may not know it is him, but it is Jesus nevertheless. Can we not suggest that when we study cosmology, geography, biology, and history—any of countless areas of study—that we, as the community of faith, are learning and/or worshiping Jesus Christ? Can we not appreciate him as designer, architect, creator, engineer, and mathematician?

This is not to say there is no place for special revelation. Scripture should hold its rightful place as the authoritative word on God and Jesus. I just want to suggest that far too many Christ followers misunderstand the freedom they have to worship Jesus wherever they see him, whether they see him in astronomy, literature, music, or anything else.

What would happen if our high school and college students understood that any area of truth belongs to Jesus Christ? When he says that he is the Truth, what does he mean (see John 14:6)? How would our churches change if we stopped acting like a group of threatened, insecure anti-intellectuals who must label all things "Christian" or "non-Christian" in order to know how to deal with them?

The fact that we don't understand and practice this freedom to proclaim truth wherever we find it and use it to point to Jesus Christ is one of the major reasons so many churched high school students turn into unchurched college students. When you are taught that the Bible is the only place one finds truth, what happens when you meet professors who do not know or love Jesus but seem to teach things that are true?

Many students either decide Christianity is a bunch of bunk or relegate following Christ (and all things religious) to the realm of "faith," while science, history, and sociology are considered the realm of "fact."

I am not saying that truth outside the Bible will never contradict truth within it. I affirm the historical testimony of the Scriptures: they are inspired and absolutely authoritative. But these inspired Scriptures also include the words of Greek poets and Cretan prophets, and they command us to love God with our minds—to test everything and claim truth wherever it is found. This is cultural engagement. It is not a matter of viewing everything found in the world as good, but neither is it viewing everything found in the world as bad. It is a matter of discernment. We must learn to test everything and hold on to the good, the redeemable, and the nourishing (see 1 Thess. 5:21).

I am also not saying that all things are true or that all viewpoints are equally good and valid. I am merely suggesting that Christ followers need not be threatened by truth outside the Bible, for all truth is a reflection of the Holy Creator God.

Consider how this would change inter-religious dialogue. We usually approach other faith traditions from an "us versus them" mentality that argues that Christians are right and all other points of view are wrong. What if, instead of leading with the idea that all of Buddhism is wrong, we began from acknowledging that there is truth in Buddhism? When Buddhists begin by saying that life is suffering and out of joint, can we not agree? Wouldn't Paul, Solomon, or Jesus say the same thing? What does it cost us to admit that we agree on the problem but disagree regarding the solution?

This is what it means to engage culture: take it on its own terms. Claim truth wherever you find it and use it to lead others to Jesus—the source of all that is good, true, and beautiful. Learn to test everything, and hold on to what is good. Labeling something "Christian" doesn't mean that it is, and simply saying something is "non-Christian" does not mean it is wholly false. Everything must be examined and tested.

This is what bothers me so much about our Christian subculture: once something is labeled "Christian," many of us simply assume it is glorifying to God and faithful to Scripture. There is a Christian radio station that proclaims itself to be "safe for the whole family." In one sense, it is—there is no vulgarity or obscenity of any kind. But I have also listened to some of the music on this station and have questions about some of the words to the songs. What attitude toward these songs am I to have as a follower of Jesus? Am I blindly to accept that because this is a "Christian" radio station these are "Christian" songs? It seems that is the implication of the labels we put on things.

Similarly, when I encounter music that Christians have labeled "secular" or "mainstream," does that mean I must assume *nothing* about it is true, good, or beautiful? Linkin Park has a song called "In the End." When I first heard it, I ran to the book of Ecclesiastes and realized these guys had nailed what life is like "under the sun"—Solomon's shorthand for life lived apart from God. Can I not claim the truth of that song, even though it is written by guys who, as far as I know, do not know and love Christ?

Keeping the Main Thing the Main Thing

One of the most pressing issues facing the early church was how to deal with the many Gentiles who were coming to faith in Jesus Christ. Some in the movement of Jesus felt Gentiles needed to obey the Law of Moses and become circumcised in order to follow Jesus. Their argument, understandably, was that Jesus was the Messiah of the Jews and, therefore, that people must become Jewish before they become Christian.

Acts 15 records for us the disagreement and the early church's response. This was the first council of the church and was not primarily a theological debate; it was about how the church should engage culture. The question at the center of this council was this: Should the church adapt itself to the new cultures it was engaging, or should the new cultures adapt themselves to the church?

The response of the council of Jerusalem is instructive for us in two ways. First, the early church affirmed the core of faith in Christ: trusting in his sacrifice alone for our salvation. Whether Jew or Gentile, all were called to trust in Jesus and nothing more was required. In everything that is secondary, the determination of the council was that the church should not make it difficult for those who do not know God to come to him. The second element of the church's response was to write to the Gentile Christians, instructing them to be sensitive to their Jewish brothers and sisters in how they expressed their faith.

What the early church did then is a model for us today. The movement of Jesus Christ has always been a center-focused movement as opposed to a boundary-focused institution.[3] The early church clarified the center of the faith in response to those who wanted to define boundaries.

To be center-focused is to emphasize the things that unite a group or organization; to be boundary-focused is to emphasize what differentiates a group or organization from other groups and organizations. Center-focused groups focus on *who we are*; boundary-focused groups focus on *who we are not*. Both the center and the boundaries must be defined to some degree for every group, but often one is emphasized over the other.

One of the reasons God calls his movement to be center-focused is because we continually need reminding that our boundaries are not necessarily his. Peter needed to be shown in a vision that Gentiles were indeed welcome into the kingdom, and Peter was even confronted by Paul when his actions were not consistent with this truth (Acts 10; Gala. 2:11–21). Jesus had to remind the disciples of this when they saw a man who was not one of them casting out demons in Jesus's name. His reply is instructive: "Do not stop him, for whoever is not against you is for you" (Luke 9:50).

Throughout the Scriptures, the people of God continually succumb to the temptation to draw the boundary lines of faith more narrowly that what God has commanded. God's boundaries are simply broader and wider and higher and deeper than ours, so he calls his followers to be marked by the center—their faith in Jesus Christ—rather than by their boundaries.

The revolution of Jesus cannot be marked off or contained within a certain theological box. As discussed earlier, movements focus on what unites; institutions focus on what divides. When Paul admits there are "disputable matters" on which sincere Christ followers may disagree, he is reminding us that there are matters that are central to the faith and matters that are peripheral (see Rom. 14:1). He is distinguishing between what is essential to faith and Christ, and what is not. He is modeling what it is to be center-focused.

At my church, Rock Harbor, this plays out in many ways. As an example, our doctrinal statement is just five statements that we believe define the center of what it means to have faith in Christ:

- God is a Trinity who exists and is the self-existent creator of all.
- Jesus is fully God and fully human; he died for our sins, rose from the dead to give us new life, and will return again.

- Human beings are created in the image of God. We have each rebelled against God's kingdom and are in need of the salvation that he alone can provide.

- God's salvation comes to us through trusting the life, death, and resurrection of Jesus and is given to us by grace alone. Nothing we can do can earn God's favor.

- The Bible is inspired by God and is authoritative over everything on which it speaks.

I share this only for purposes of illustration. Without debating the exact wording, we are convinced by the Scriptures that this is the core of faith in Jesus. We don't have an "official" position on issues like the millennium or who we think may be the anti-Christ. We recognize these as important areas of study, but we also recognize and respect that many in our congregation hold diverse views. We hold a similar position regarding the gifts of the Spirit. Some in our church are convinced that speaking in tongues is a gift still given today; others believe some gifts ceased once the Bible was put together. In response, we agree with Paul, "Each one should be fully convinced in his own mind" (Rom. 14:5). We would never break fellowship with someone who disagreed over these issues—they are not central or essential to what it means to follow Jesus.

Thus, we seek to continually define and reinforce the center of our faith. This means that when we talk with those outside the community of faith in Jesus, we don't fight every battle. My faith in Jesus doesn't hinge on whether Jonah was really swallowed by a whale. Personally, I happen to think he was, because Jesus seemed to refer to this incident as real and historical. But if my opinion were somehow disproved, my faith in Jesus would remain untouched. The early church tied everything to the resurrection of Jesus (see 1 Cor. 15:12–32). That was the cornerstone of their faith.

As we seek to engage and redeem culture, this is worth keeping in mind. Only the central core of our faith is worth dying for. That is the only part we should spend time or risk relationships defending. Whether or not the flood was global or local has very little to do with someone outside the faith stepping into God's kingdom. Our view of the tribulation is of little concern to the world around us. What matters is that we present Jesus of Nazareth as faithfully as we can. He will take care of the rest.

10

SHOW AND TELL

One of the reasons I ended up following Jesus is that he made so many things in my life make sense. I had an agnostic, culturally Jewish, philosophy professor my sophomore year in college. He and I hit it off, and I got to spend some time with him in his office talking about the "deep" things in life. I once asked him why he wasn't a Christian. He responded by reeling off a list of intellectual objections he had to belief in God in general and Christianity in particular. He didn't think the believers in God had proven God's existence. He questioned the idea that God was good in light of the evil of the world. He was skeptical of the line of thought that led to the claim that the Bible was inspired by God.

His objections were so powerful and persuasive that I gave up what little faith I had. My church had never taught me how to answer these questions, and I had never thought to ask them. My college experience up until that point had already been confusing enough; I was coming into contact with professors and students, from various disciplines, who were great people and whose views made sense. I had been taught that truth didn't exist outside of Christianity: if it wasn't in the Bible, then it wasn't worth believing. So I was faced with the dilemma of being intellectually honest or following Jesus. I hadn't yet learned that I could do both.

In response to my professor's objections, I began to read people like C. S. Lewis and Josh McDowell—people who argued that following Jesus was an intelligent thing to do. Over the course of several years, I learned that there were good answers to my professor's questions and good reasons why Jesus was worth giving my life to. I talked with Buddhists and atheists, discussed life with feminists and naturalists, and learned a great deal about what other people believed and why they believed what they did.

I became fascinated by the branch of Christian thought called *apologetics*—the intellectual defense of the Christian faith. For me, this study was quite helpful, and I learned that you didn't have to be an idiot to believe in Jesus.

But the longer I have followed Jesus and the more I have observed the changes occurring in the culture around us, I am convinced that the modern approaches to defending Christianity are becoming increasingly irrelevant. They are still helpful, but issues like the existence of God, the possibility of miracles, and the inspiration of the Bible are no longer the primary objections people have to faith in Christ. In fact,

I have observed that it is people inside the church, who want to grow and strengthen their faith, who are the principal consumers of apologetic lectures and books. Most of those outside the faith are no longer asking these questions.

There is nothing wrong, of course, with Christians seeking and finding answers to hard questions about what faith in Jesus means and why someone should have it. It definitely helped me. But my concern is that we have moved from speaking a language and addressing issues that are relevant to those outside the community of faith to focusing instead on strengthening those who are already convinced.

The most common (and powerful) objections to faith in Jesus are no longer intellectual, per se, but rather are *moral* in nature. In other words, the predominant questions culture was asking fifty years ago were intellectual questions: Has evolution disproved creation? Does God exist? Can miracles happen? What are the proofs for the resurrection of Christ?

In response, the Christian community focused on answering these questions: here are many different arguments that prove the existence of God, here are refutations of Darwinism, and here are historical arguments that prove the validity of the Bible and resurrection of Jesus.[1] All of this was valuable and has led to the resurgence of Christian faith in Western academia.

But the culture around us has ceased asking these questions. We are spending our time answering concerns that very few people outside the church are wondering about. Sociologists comment regularly on the universality of religious belief.

Spirituality and belief in something higher than ourselves have never been more popular. Books like *Conversations with God* reveal that we are comfortable with the idea of God speaking to and through ordinary people. The current focus on angels, demons, and the supernatural pervade the publishing and entertainment industries. Indeed, many people are accepting of Jesus but are suspicious of organized religion.

Today's challenges to followers of Jesus come in an increasingly moral form. Why can't two gay men who love each other marry? What is wrong with experimenting on stem cells harvested through aborted fetuses? How can Christians claim that their religion is the only correct one and that everyone else is damned to hell? In all of these debates, the Christian position is typically portrayed as the *least moral* position![2] Followers of Jesus, so the argument goes, are narrow-minded, hypocritical bigots and homophobes who do nothing but push their agenda on people in any way possible.

These are their moral arguments against us: It is more *loving* to accept gay marriage, it is more *just* to allow stem cell research and abortion on demand, and it is more *tolerant* to uphold the religious convictions of people outside the Christian faith. People want to know why they should trust the Bible when it has been interpreted so many different ways (it has been used by white supremacists to justify their position, slave owners to justify slavery, and men to justify the second-class status of women). They want to know why they should go to church when the lives of the people they find there bear no noticeable difference from the way they themselves live (some interesting statistics on this can be found at George Barna's Web site: http://www.barna.org).[3] They look at our hypocrisy and wonder why they should give up their Sunday mornings. As Brian McLaren has pointed out, many people have concerns "not about truth of Christianity, but rather about the goodness of it."[4]

My contention is that modern apologetic approaches to defending Christianity are not answering these objections effectively. In a society where any claims of universality, rationality, and objectivity are suspect from the outset, the Christian must first persuade its audience that Christianity has something important to say and should be heard; only then should we suggest that it might be true.

This brings us to the most important principle of all in redeeming our culture: *demonstrating* the message of Christ. Matthew 4:23 says, "Jesus went throughout Galilee, teaching in their synagogues, preaching the good news of the kingdom, and healing every disease and sickness among the people."

Many scholars divide the ministry of Christ into the "proclamation" and the "demonstration" of the message of the kingdom. In other words, Jesus didn't simply announce the good news of the kingdom of God; he embodied that news as well. Through his compassionate miracles, authoritative teaching, and perfect moral life, Jesus represented the reality of his message.

If it is true that most objections to Christianity are becoming moral in nature, then perhaps it is time to reexamine the "demonstration" part of the ministry of Jesus. Much good work has been done on how to proclaim the message (the tools of evangelism), what message to proclaim (theology and doctrine), and the defense of the message of Christ (the study of apologetics). But less has been done on what it looks like to embody the message of Jesus as we share it. This, the demonstration of the gospel, is now as critical as proclamation.

In both Acts 10 and Galatians 1, Peter needed to be reminded of not just the message of Jesus but also the *way* of Jesus. We need reminding, too. We need to recall the profound and simple power of the gospel put on display through the lives of ordinary people. What does this demonstration look like as we seek to redeem culture? Again, Jesus shows us the way.

Can I Get a Witness?

It is often suggested that evangelism is something we "do" when we "share" our faith with someone outside the Christian community. Apologetics is said to be that branch of evangelism that deals with answering objections and presenting evidence for the truth of the Christian gospel. So we in the church "send" missionaries to do the sharing for us, and we "equip" those who are interested to answer tough questions.

The problem is that Scripture teaches that we don't *send* missionaries; we *are* missionaries, some of whom are sent.

As Paul declares in 2 Corinthians 5:20, "We are therefore Christ's ambassadors, as though God were making his appeal through us."⁵ The main issue with the traditional understanding of evangelism and apologetics is that they are too narrowly construed. The Bible teaches that evangelism is life (we *are* salt and light) and that the greatest apologetic is a life lived in obedience to God.

Who, then, are the best missionaries, the best demonstrators of the gospel? The pastors? No way. We're "paid" to be religious. I think it is the mortgage brokers, moms, students, janitors, baristas, and executives who fill our churches. How does God reach lawyers? By dressing up some of his children as lawyers and putting them to work. How does God reach college students? By dressing up his children as college students and sending them off to school. As Jesus put it in Matthew 28:19, As you are going through life, "make disciples of all nations."

You are not only a priest with a spiritual calling to ministry (in whatever you do), but also a full-time missionary whose job it is to put the message of Jesus on display by how you live. Many times we are called to use words in doing this, but often it is simply a matter of living the revolution. You don't need special training for this (although it would never hurt us); you need only the grace and power of God's Spirit within you and the courageous willingness to engage those people God puts around you. Remember, people can't help but talk about what they love and enjoy in life, whether it is a car, job, relationship, or hobby. If someone is passionate about the environment, I can't talk to that person for very long without hearing about it. If one of my single friends has a new girlfriend, I don't have to ask many questions in order to find out about her. Why is it any different about a person who is passionate for Jesus? Why do so many approaches to "sharing our faith" seem so awkward and contrived? Could it be because, instead of sharing our faith, we should just be sharing our lives—of which our faith is the defining part? What if we understood that our role as missionaries is to put Jesus on display in a thousand ways simply by living our lives?

Of course there is a time to speak, to defend, to answer questions, and to present reasons. But we too often look to specialists for that. We have lost the art of conversation and asking good, thought-provoking questions. We have ceased operating from a place of strength and security as we seek to engage others with Jesus. We need to see our role as missionaries—right where we are, doing just what we do.

Followers of the Way

I find it interesting to note that the earliest Christians were not only known as believers but also known as followers. Specifically, Acts 9:2 and 24:14 refer to the followers of Jesus as followers of the Way. They were known for their way of life. For them, following Christ wasn't just an exercise in believing, but in living. Their beliefs caused them to live in certain ways. Today we are known primarily for what we believe, not what we do. Ask anyone outside the Christian community what they think of when they hear the word *Christian*, and they will most likely give you a list of political views (prolife, antihomosexual) or moral pejoratives (hypocrites, narrow minded, intolerant). Grace, compassion, mercy, or love probably won't be on the list.

This is how far we have come. During the first two centuries, Christian writers arguing for the truth of Christianity would point to the acts of love and compassion evidenced by the church. These days, arguments for Christianity center on the removal of intellectual doubts and addressing felt needs. Following Jesus is primarily about just that: following. Not just saying or singing or trying. Not just talking a good spiritual game. But actually, through God's grace, loving as Jesus loved, living as Jesus lived, and teaching as Jesus taught. We seem to have made the whole thing an intellectual exercise in being "right."

John points this out in his Gospel: "Jesus did many other miraculous signs in the presence of his disciples, which are not recorded in this book. But these are written that you may believe that Jesus is the Christ, the Son of God, and that by believing you may have life in his name" (John 20:30–31). For John, believing was not the goal; it was the means, not the end. The goal was living a certain kind of life oriented to the teachings of Jesus (what Jesus called being a disciple); believing certain things about God led you into this life. For John, believing leads to living.[6]

The reason this is so important is that everybody follows somebody.[7] We all learn how to live and love from somebody else. By listening and observing, I can learn whom someone is following, and, I hope, they will see in me someone following Jesus Christ. It seems that we have quit seeing Jesus as a teacher and rabbi and have made him into being only a savior and for-giver. As we have seen, Jesus calls me to surrender my whole life into his hands and promises to teach me how to live in his king-dom. As I learn to live my life as if Jesus had my life to live, I put him on display to those around me.[8] Because we all follow somebody, the best demonstration of the good news of Jesus is for people outside the kingdom of Jesus to see what happens when you follow him.

Giving Ourselves Away

This way of living was to be completely counter to the cul-ture around it. In Mark 10:42–44, Jesus distinguishes between how the larger dominant culture of the world oper-ates and how things are to be in his kingdom: "You know that those who are regarded as rulers of the Gentiles lord it over them, and their high officials exercise authority over them. Not so with you. Instead, whoever wants to become great among you must be your servant, and whoever wants to be first must be slave of all."

With those outside his kingdom, Jesus said, it is all about climbing the ladder and stepping on anyone who gets in your way. But he called his disciples to another way: the way of giving and serving. Our posture toward each other and the culture around us, then, is diametrically opposed to the culture itself. How do we redeem culture? We observe it and engage it on its terms and then demonstrate the message of Jesus through service and love.

Jesus continues in that same passage: "For even the Son of Man did not come to be served, but to serve, and to give his life as a ransom for many" (v. 45). Jesus connects the approach of his movement to culture to how *he* sought to redeem it. Instead of waiting behind our church walls for those hardy "seekers" brave enough to enter our doors, Jesus calls us to go out and serve the lost and broken communities around us. He went after lost people—he pursued them. He didn't always wait for people to come to him first (see Luke 19:10). This revolution of kindness was in direct opposition to the powers of the world.

We could point to many examples of this kind of engagement with the world. One of the most striking is the story of Craig Gross and Mike Foster and their quest to redeem the porn industry.[9] Founders of xxxchurch.com, these two men have withstood withering criticism from within the Christian community for their attempts to reach out to the purveyors (and the victims) of the multibillion-dollar pornography empire. They attend porn conventions (with their wives, no less), handing out "Jesus loves porn stars" T-shirts and challenging people to go without porn for seven days. They even inaugurated a "porn Sunday" in 2005 for churches around the United States to call their congregations to wake up to the reality of porn and porn addiction in their midst.

I don't know these men personally or know all that they attempt to do in fulfilling the call God has placed upon them. But I can say without a doubt that I have benefited personally from their ministry (their accountability software is on my computer) and admire their courage in seeking to bring the light and life of Jesus into the darkest of places. They didn't wait for the lost to come to them—they went to where those people were and demonstrated the grace and truth of the gospel with their actions.

The church exists to serve the world around it. That is our fundamental orientation. As followers of Jesus, we no longer exist for ourselves. We must constantly resist the inertia that pulls the church inward—focusing on its own comfort, safety, prosperity, and success. We rebel against a culture that defines greatness as power and prestige, and proclaim instead that greatness is found in giving ourselves away. The church of Jesus should have nothing to do with entitlement, manipulation, control, or arrogance. Instead, we should be seeking how we can serve and love each other and the world.

Living the Way of Jesus, then, orients us away from the dominant sway of culture. We, as an act of loving rebellion, position ourselves to demonstrate the gospel through humble service. This is what God has always asked of his followers. He blessed Israel so they would be a blessing to others. We are shown mercy and forgiveness so we may show mercy and forgiveness to others. That is why James defines true religion as looking after orphans and widows (James 1:27). That is why God looks at Israel's worship in Isaiah 1 and announces that he hates it and it makes him sick. Israel's worship was devoid of justice for the oppressed, the fatherless, and the widow (see Isa. 1:11–17). On another occasion, God rejects Israel's fasting because justice and service did not accompany it:

> Is not this the kind of fasting I have chosen: to loose the chains of injustice and untie the cords of the yoke, to set the oppressed free and break every yoke? Is it not to share your food with the hungry and to provide the poor wanderer with shelter—when you see the naked, to clothe him, and not to turn away from your own flesh and blood? (Isa. 58:6–7)

This is why Jesus, in Matthew 25:3–26, reminds us that we are accountable for how we serve the world around us. The Scriptures declare in a multitude of ways that believing well is important (by believing, we become children of God) but that it is nothing if it is divorced from living well. Jesus never talks about our accountability to him in terms of whether or not we believed well. His judgment is always based on how well we lived what we believed. Certainly, we must believe, and belief is central to action. But it never stops there. Biblical faith is always translated into our love of and service to those around us. Faith without deeds is dead, James tells us (James 2:14–26). John announces that if we claim to love God yet hate others, we are liars and the truth of God is not in us (1 John 3:1–21; 4:7–21). Luke reminds us that in the early church, "there were no needy persons among them" (Acts 4:32–35).

It is one thing to argue for a pro-life position. It is another thing to adopt AIDS children and serve as foster parents. It is one thing to proclaim that God loves everybody. It is another thing to minister to rapists in prison. It is one thing to argue that Jesus can change your life. It is another thing entirely to show you the change in my own.

I'm inspired by the many college students in our church who take what are called the "best years" of their lives and spend them on the poor, the needy, and the outcasts. When a team from our church recently left on a two-week mission trip to India, a young woman among them was making a one-way trip. She intends to stay for three years (maybe more) and minister to prostitutes and sex slaves.

What would happen if such giving began to characterize our churches? What would happen if we took the best of our resources and refused to spend them on ourselves but instead invested them in making the world a better reflection of Jesus? What would happen? People need to see what we are for, not just what we are against. So much of our message is tied to what the Christian community opposes: Harry Potter, homosexual marriage, abortion, feminism, stem-cell research, et cetera. But what are we *for*? The world needs to know we stand for faith, hope, love, truth, beauty, grace, compassion, kindness, and courage. The only way they will know is if we show them. Words, these days, are meaningless.

This, then, is the ultimate apologetic: the demonstration of the message of Jesus through the posture of service and love. Of course we need intelligent thinkers and articulate answers. But the Bible calls us to show *and* tell. So much of the movements in evangelism are focused solely on the telling; I argue that Scripture puts as much, if not more, emphasis on the showing. There's no dismissing a transformed life.

Therefore, any response from the community of Jesus to the culture around us must take these things into account in order to be effective. Even if we could unequivocally prove that God indeed exists and can be shown rationally, the inhabitants of our culture would yawn and return to their pagan slumber. What our world seems to be waiting for is not more incessant talk about objective truth but an embodied witness that clearly demonstrates why anyone should care about Jesus in the first place. Most of our non-Christian neighbors cannot pick us out as different from the rest of their non-Christian neighbors. This fact alone suggests that they are right in refusing to accept what we say we believe but which our lives make a lie.

Thus, we may be willing, as 1 Peter 3:15 suggests, to give the reason for that hope that we have, but the problem is that no one seems to be asking. Unless we are content to answer questions that no one is posing, then our most urgent task is to live in such a way that compels others to ask us about the hope that we have.

I want to help create a new kind of community that meets real needs and subverts the culture around it. I pray that my son will grow up to see that biblical masculinity is found in Jesus and that my son exists to give himself away for something bigger than a paycheck. I pray my daughter will grow up in a community that both tells her and shows her that she does not have to be perfect to be beautiful, that reminds her that she is lovely and delightful just as she is. I pray to be a part of a community where the reality of the risen Jesus isn't just lofty theological ideas and concepts but expresses itself in a million different ways in order to reshape individuals and the cultures in which they live.

The purpose of the church isn't just to survive this world but to become dynamic movements who live out the revolution of Jesus. We are called to serve and love the world around us. It is understandable why many do not want to do so. The world is ugly, fallen, and depraved. It is far easier to close ourselves off to the messiness of culture and focus on preserving our traditions and rituals. It is far easier to divide ourselves according to our theological distinctions (which no longer matter to people outside the church, by the way) than to focus on what unites us so we can mobilize together as the greater community of faith.

Just as individual disciples find their lives by losing them, so, too, the church lives by dying to its preferences, comfort, and safety. As a religion, Christianity is no better or worse than the other great religions of the world. But as a revolution, it is something else (and far better) entirely. May the church cease being seen as religious communities and start becoming the revolutionary movement God intended.

Conclusion

I have heard it said that nothing is more dangerous to a revolution than winning. When a revolution wins, it faces the prospect of becoming institutionalized and losing its ability to be dangerous and subversive. If there is nothing to revolt against, a revolution loses its power. Revolutions are by nature subversive.

For instance, where in the world is the global church dead? In places where Christianity is the state religion. Where does it flourish? Where it is persecuted and oppressed. It would seem that if the opponents of Christ in the United States really wanted to stop the movement of Jesus, all they would have to do is to make Christianity the national religion. The separation of church and state actually protects us from winning in our desire to turn America into a "Christian nation." God save us from such a fate. In the Scriptures, past success is always the greatest threat to future usefulness in God's kingdom (reference, for example, the story of Uzziah in 2 Chron. 26). We lose the ability to be useful in God's hands when we become afraid to lose the success we have achieved.

As I have said, the fundamental mistake the Western church makes as it relates to the world is to assume the problems of the church are the result of the increasing hostility and secularization of the culture around us. But I have argued that the problem is not outside the church, but inside. As we lose sight of the subversive and revolutionary Jesus of Nazareth, we become progressively more accommodating to culture. Instead of influencing and shaping the world around us, the church is reflecting our cultural ideas and values to a greater and greater degree. As Erwin McManus points out,

> From athlete to actor, musician to politician, both those who advocate the heart of God and those who seem to war against him have many times been the product of the Western church. The problem has not been that these individuals of significant influence were outside the sphere of the church's influence, but that, in fact, they sat at the center of the church and remained unchanged at the core.
>
> America's best atheists are children of the church. It is rare to find a person who is a passionate enemy of the church who has never had contact with her. The diminishing influence of the American church on American society is not simply because fewer people are going to church, but fewer people are going to church because of the diminishing influence of Christ on the church itself. . . . People are rejecting Christ *because* of the church![10]

The reason Christ has had diminishing influence on the church is because the church has accepted a diminished Christ.

The Jesus of Suburbia is the Jesus of Christian religion. He is the Jesus who calls us into comfort and convenience and away from engaging the world around us with truth and grace. He is the Jesus who is understandable and clear cut. He is the Jesus who makes sense. Not surprisingly, we are tempted to follow him. The children of God have always been tempted to temper and soften the God who is there into a much tamer counterfeit.

The great nineteenth-century London preacher Charles Spurgeon, when asked how he defended the word of God, responded that he defended it the same way he would defend a lion, simply by letting it out of its cage. This book is an exploration of the many ways we may box in Jesus and a call to let him loose. We have settled for something other than the real Christ; we have settled for a far smaller and safer version.

The Scriptures remind us, time and again, that the more you know God, the bigger he gets. For us in the Western church, often the opposite is true. The more we get to know him, the more we think we have him figured out. We become accustomed to a faith of tips and techniques, and we forget the terrifying exhilaration of abandoning ourselves to Jesus.

The Bible repeatedly reminds us of this paradox: we can know God, but we can never figure him out. I don't understand him, but I can know him and enter into relationship with him. It is this paradox that allows us to live with confidence (we know that Jesus is good, powerful, and loving) and reverent fear (we know that he is holy and awesome—he is simply beyond our understanding). The joy of following Christ comes precisely because we know him well enough to know that we'll never know him fully.

It is this thrill of discovery that keeps the movement of Jesus from becoming stale and institutional.

Have you ever thought you knew something (or someone) only to find out there was much, much more? Maybe you thought you knew your spouse (until you married him or her) or your friend (until you became roommates) or your child (until he or she hit puberty).

I have a friend who took his five-year-old to Disneyland for the first time. Once through the gates, there is a relatively small area where pictures are taken with costumed characters and you can hear the sounds of the Disneyland Express. The park lies beyond this picture area, but my friend's son didn't know that. When he tried to take his son away from the characters and into the park beyond, the boy howled in protest, convinced that his dad was forcing him to leave the park. The little boy had assumed that where he was standing was the extent of the park. Imagine the joy and thrill when his dad dragged him around the corner into Disneyland itself and he realized what he thought was the park wasn't the park at all, but only the beginning. Imagine the joy of knowing that you have *all day* to explore this place with your dad.

I experienced the same thing with the Grand Canyon. If you'll remember, my brother and I were content to swim at the campgrounds out West instead of going to see the incredible sights. Even as we parked at Grand Canyon National Park, I couldn't figure out what all the fuss was about. Isn't a canyon just a hole in the ground? Imagine my shock when I walked through the Ranger Station and out to the Rim. I couldn't believe it. I just stood there for half an hour trying to take it all in.

Have you ever thought you knew Jesus Christ, only to find out that there is much more to him?

This has been my experience with Jesus of Nazareth. Each time I think I have him pinned down, he does something to remind me how big he really is. The danger comes when we think we understand him, when we box him in so that he makes sense. This is what kills the joy of discovery and the anticipation of pursuit. What keeps him from getting bigger? Only the idea that I have him figured out. What drives our pursuit of Jesus is the paradox of knowing him yet understanding we'll never comprehend him.

How sad would it be for the people of God to lose their wonder and joy in pursing Jesus? How sad would it be for the people of God to substitute their knowledge of Jesus for actually knowing him? Maybe you've been to Bible studies and church services often enough to think you know him. Maybe you've grown bored with the revolution because you've heard it all before in youth group and summer camp. Or maybe this is all new to you. Wherever you are in your faith journey, the one thing I want for both of us is this: I want us to get a glimpse of Jesus—as he really is, not as we want him to be. Just one glimpse of him, in his majesty and glory, and we'll never be the same.

Would you ask the Jesus of Nazareth (not the false Jesus of the church or of American suburbia) to show himself to you in unmistakable ways? This is a dangerous request. I believe it is one Jesus always answers. He reveals himself to people whose hearts are open. Let us throw down our idols and vending machine gods and give Jesus Christ his rightful place as Lord and King in both our hearts and our churches.

Notes

Chapter 1

1. C. S. Lewis, *The Weight of Glory* © C. S. Lewis Pte. Ltd. 2001, Extract reprinted by permission.

2. The main idea for this chapter was shaped by a book Rob Bell recommended: Richard A. Horsley, *The Liberation of Christmas* (New York: Crossroad Publishing, 1989). For more information about Caesar Augustus, I recommend Richard A. Horsley, *Jesus and Empire* (Minneapolis: Fortress Press, 2003); Werner Eck, *The Age of Augustus*, trans. Deborah Lucas Schneider (Malden, MA: Blackwell Publishing, 2003); John Dominic Crossan and Jonathan L. Reed, *In Search of Paul: How Jesus' Apostle Opposed Rome's Empire with God's Kingdom* (New York: HarperSanFrancisco, 2004); Paul Zanker, *The Power of Images in the Age of Augustus*, trans. Alan Shapiro (Ann Arbor: University of Michigan Press, 1988); Richard J. Cassidy, *Christians and Roman Rule in the New Testament* (New York: Crossroad Publishing, 2001); Will Durant, *Caesar and Christ* (New York: Simon and Schuster, 1944); Thomas Cahill, *Desire of the Everlasting Hills* (New York:

Anchor Books, 1999); Richard A. Horsley and Neil Asher Silberman, *The Message and the Kingdom: How Jesus and Paul Ignited a Revolution and Transformed the Ancient World* (Minneapolis: Fortress Press, 2002).

3. Reed, *In Search of Paul*, 91.

4. Horsley, *Jesus and Empire*, 23–24.

5. Reed, *In Search of Paul*, 206.

6. For some further study on Herod, consult Richard A. Horsley, *The Liberation of Christmas* (New York: Crossroad Publishing, 1989); Peter Richardson, *Herod: King of the Jews and Friend of the Romans* (Minneapolis: Fortress Press, 1999); Duane W. Roller, *The Building Program of Herod the Great* (Los Angeles: University of California Press, 1998); and also Ray VanderLaan, http://www.followtherabbi.com.

7. Rob Bell, unpublished sermon.

Chapter 2

1. Erwin Raphael McManus, *An Unstoppable Force: Daring to Become the Church God Had in Mind* (Loveland, CO: Group Publishing, 2001), 32–33.

2. John Eldredge expands on this point in his book, *Waking the Dead* (Nashville, TN: Thomas Nelson Publishers, 2003), 3–35.

3. This point was inspired by an unpublished teaching from Erwin McManus.

Chapter 3

1. Philip Yancey, *The Jesus I Never Knew* (Grand Rapids, MI: Zondervan Publishing House, 1995).

2. Tim Keller, "Religion-Less Spirituality," *Leadership Journal* 20, no. 4 (Fall 1999): 25.

3. To survey: Islam mandates five pillars that must be followed to enter into paradise. The twin Hindu doctrines of karma and reincarnation focus on one's religious performance over the course of many lifetimes. Buddhism offers the eight-fold path to enlightenment. All religious systems, from the globally recognized to small regional cults, have this in common. They are ladders one must climb to reach heaven/nirvana/paradise. I argue that much of what passes as Christianity is the same thing: empty religion disguised as the teachings of Jesus.

4. *Shalom* is a rich Hebrew word. It goes further than simple peace. It connotes wholeness and health of the sort intended in the Garden of Eden.

5. Dallas Willard, *The Divine Conspiracy: Rediscovering Our Hidden Life in God* (New York: HarperSanFrancisco, 1998), 139–44.

Chapter 4

1. For an excellent treatment on the temple, see Alfred Edersheim, *The Temple: Its Ministry and Services*, rev. ed. (Peabody, MA: Hendrickson Publishers, 1994).

2. Ron Moseley, *Yeshua: A Guide to the Real Jesus and the Original Church* (Baltimore, MD: Lederer Books, 1996), 112.

3. Bart Tarman, from an unpublished sermon.

4. See Paul Brand and Philip Yancey, *Fearfully and Wonderfully Made* (Grand Rapids, MI: Zondervan, 1997).

Chapter 5

1. This analogy of the distinction between knowing God and knowing about God comes from J. I. Packer, *Knowing God*, 20th Anniversary Ed. (Downers Grove, IL: InterVarsity Press, 1993), 25–26.

2. For a scathing indictment of the evangelical church in America, see Ronald J. Sider, *The Scandal of the Evangelical Conscience* (Grand Rapids, MI: Baker Books, 2005).

3. Mark Buchanan, *The Holy Wild: Trusting in the Character of God* (Sisters, OR: Multnoman, 2005), 29.

4. Rob Bell, "Show, Don't Tell," unpublished sermon.

Chapter 6

1. This chapter is largely indebted to Michael E. Wittmer, *Heaven Is a Place on Earth* (Grand Rapids, MI: Zondervan, 2004).

2. See Cornelius Plantinga Jr., *Engaging God's World* (Grand Rapids, MI: William B. Eerdmans Publishing Company, 2002), 22–28.

3. See Brother Lawrence, *The Practice of the Presence of God* (New Kensington, PA: Whitaker House, 1982).

4. Wittmer, *Heaven*, 55–59.

5. Excerpt is from *God was in This Place and I, I Did Not Know: Finding Self, Spirituality, and Ultimate Meaning* © 1994 Lawrence Kushner (Woodstock, VT: Jewish Lights Publishing). Permission granted by Jewish Lights Publishing, P.O. Box 237, Woodstock, VT 05091 www.jewishlights.com.

Chapter 7

1. See http://maggidawn.typepad.com.

2. Perhaps this is why we possess no physical description of Jesus: we would elevate that image. Or it is the reason we don't have the original manuscripts of the Bible: we would revere those instead of the God behind them. Idolatry has always been the temptation of the people of God.

3. We know him in English as Jesus. Jesus is derived from the Hebrew Ye'shua, which means "YHWH saves"—how cool is that!

Chapter 8

1. See also Gordon D. Fee and Douglas Stuart, *How to Read the Bible for All Its Worth*, 2nd ed. (Grand Rapids, MI: Zondervan, 1993), 231–38.

2. Marcus Borg, *The Heart of Christianity* (New York: HarperSanFrancisco, 2003), 136–37; see also Craig S. Keener, *The NIV Application Commentary: Revelation* (Grand Rapids, MI: Zondervan, 2000); G. K. Beale, *The New International Greek Testament Commentary: The Book of Revelation* (Grand Rapids, MI: William B. Eerdmans Publishing Company, 1999); Grant R. Osborne, *Baker Exegetical Commentary on the New Testament: Revelation* (Grand Rapids, MI: Baker Academic, 2002); for a different perspective on the book of Revelation, see Peter Hiett, *Eternity Now!: Encountering the Jesus of Revelation* (Nashville, TN: Integrity Publishers, 2003).

3. Richard Bauckham, *The Theology of the Book of Revelation* (Cambridge, UK: Cambridge University Press, 1993).

Chapter 9

1. Mark Driscoll, *The Radical Reformission: Reaching Out Without Selling Out* (Grand Rapids, MI: Zondervan, 2004), 56–57; Donald Guthrie, *New Testament Introduction* (Downers Grove, IL: InterVarsity Press, 1990).

2. Rob Bell, *Velvet Elvis: Repainting the Christian Faith* (Grand Rapids, MI: Zondervan, 2005), 79–80.

3. I first encountered this distinction in Leighton Ford, *Transforming Leadership* (Downers Grove, IL: InterVarsity Press, 1991), 211.

Chapter 10

1. For example: J. P. Moreland and Kai Nielson, *Does God Exist?: The Debate Between Theists and Atheists* (Amherst, NY: Prometheus Books, 1990); Phillip E. Johnson, *Darwin on Trial* (Downers Grove, IL: InterVarsity Press, 1993); Josh McDowell, *The New Evidence That Demands a Verdict* (Nashville, TN: Nelson Reference, 1999).

2. John Piper and Justin Taylor, eds., *Sex and the Supremacy of Christ* (Wheaton, IL: Crossway Books, 2005), 14.

3. Ron Sider, *The Scandal of the Evangelical Conscience* (Grand Rapids, MI: Baker Books, 2005).

4. Taken from *More Ready Than You Realize* by Brian D. McLaren. Copyright © 2002 By Brian D. McLaren. Used by permission of The Zondervan Corporation.

5. The rest of the chapter is an amazing call for all of us to adopt something Paul calls the "ministry of reconciliation," which I call "demonstration."

6. Rob Bell makes this point beautifully in an unpublished sermon, "Show, Don't Tell."

7. Dallas Willard, *The Divine Conspiracy: Rediscovering Our Hidden Life in God* (New York: HarperSanFrancisco, 1998), 271.

8. Ibid., 283.

9. Their story is told in Craig Gross, *The Gutter: Where Life Is Meant to Be Lived* (Orlando, FL: Relevant Books, 2005).

10. Erwin Raphael McManus, *An Unstoppable Force: Daring to Become the Church God Had in Mind* (Loveland, CO: Group Publishing, 2001), 28–29.